Accessing God-Ordained Rooms

The Blessing of Miraculous Happenings

Maureen Manoly

Unless otherwise noted, all scriptures are taken from the King James version of the Bible.

Accessing God Ordained Rooms: The Blessing of Miraculous Happenings

ISBN: 979-8-89034-621-6

Cover Design by Lex Design

Editor: Blaze Hawkins

Printed in the United States of America.

DEDICATION

I dedicate this book to my Pastor and Senior
Covenant Leader of twelve years and
counting, Apostle Dr. G. Marie Carroll. Her
love for God, purity, obedience, and
steadfastness have paved the way for me to
access many God-ordained rooms locally and
globally. Her first impartation over my life
twelve years ago was teaching me how to
access the Throne Room through worship
and prayer. My life has totally changed for the
better since the LORD called us both into
apostolic covenant.

ACKNOWLEGEMENTS

My gratitude is to God, my Father and Creator, for affording me the grace to release His thoughts on paper. Your plans are good and always lead to an expected end! I honor, adore, and love you, Heavenly Father.

I thank the Holy Spirit, the author and writer par excellence, for leading me into writing this book so quickly. What an amazing teacher you are! My life has been transformed ever since I fully received you.

Jesus, my champion, and intercessor in Heaven, how I adore you for showing me the way, and for reminding me that it is possible to bring you with me in and out of rooms to bring Heaven on Earth.

I am eternally thankful for my parents Jean-Hermann and Marie Christine Bruno Manoly as well as my sisters Maevis Pierre and Mearrha Apollon for their faithful love, prayers, and support.

I wish to thank my mentor and friend Etude Amielle Pierre, BSN for over twenty years of friendship and wisdom: Amie, you inspire me to become better every day and above all to follow the leading of the Holy Spirit. Thank you for being a major catalyst in my life as God prepared me to access many rooms. I love you!

This book became a reality because of the excellent wisdom, apostolic insight, and skills of my Pastor Apostle Dr. G. Marie Carroll, my friend and editor Blaze Hawkins, and Lex Design: one of the most talented designers that I know.

My gratitude is extended to my friends, mentors, mentees, ministry partners, church family, and other giants in the body of Christ who have taught me and are yet teaching me the value of bringing Jesus and the Holy Spirit inside and outside of the rooms ordained by Him for His glory. Thank you for your total surrender to Christ and His mission, and your tireless efforts towards advancing His Kingdom in the earth.

FOREWORD BY APOSTLE

G. MARIE CARROLL

Being in the room where it happens is
of the utmost importance. I believe that
Apostle Maureen Manoly has captured the
essence of Psalm 16:11, where David
expressed the importance of the presence of
God as a game changer. Psalm 16:11 states,
"Thou wilt shew me the path of life: in thy
presence is fulness of joy; at thy right hand
there are pleasures for evermore" (King James
Version 1769/2017, Psalm 16:11).

This book is sure to invite you into
the room where miracles signs and wonders

reside! Apostle Maureen Manoly is using sound doctrine to demonstrate the power of being in right relationship with God and how that relationship will always open doors to rooms of purpose, power and presence that will prevail as one continues in communion with the one and only true God, Jesus Christ our Lord and Savior! I am encouraged by reading this work and I am sure you will also benefit from the prophetic decrees that are written here!

TABLE OF CONTENTS

CHAPTER 1

THE PURPOSE OF ROOMS

It was a beautiful afternoon in January 2023, and I was in a beautiful room adorned with flowers, chandeliers, and light. Everyone there was looking forward to the processional and entrance of the bride and groom. As the music was playing in the background and I vaguely listened to the chatter around me, the Holy Spirit quietly whispered to me: "Maureen, you are in the room".

Excited and puzzled, I looked up for a moment and smiled. I did not ask Him what He meant by that statement. I knew that more would be revealed to me later. So, I simply sat back, looked around, observed, and enjoyed the moment.

During the reception later that evening, I was surrounded by influential people in the Kingdom and worldwide. The wedding and reception took place in different rooms, and again, I felt drawn to watch and observe others while in the room. The wedding was that of Prophetess Sophia Ruffin and her husband Tommy Wilson. It was a glorious gathering! Two days later, the Holy Spirit unveiled more on God's purpose and plans of placing His chosen ones in rooms for His glory. God desires for us to maximize His

2

plan as He grants us access to rooms where it is happening!

According to Merriam-Webster's online dictionary, a room is "an extent of space occupied by or sufficient or available for something; a suitable or fit occasion or opportunity". A room is often located within a building or other architectural structure, and it is often covered and given access to through doors and windows. Rooms are designed for a variety of purposes: boardrooms are where business meetings take place among executives and staff, dining rooms are designed to house members of a family or friends to share a meal, a courtroom is the appointed location ruled by a judge and where legal proceedings take place, and a supply room is the place assigned by office managers to store office supplies. Each room has a specific purpose and is designed by the architect with the intent of the room in mind.

As we delve further into the various rooms highlighted in Scripture and Jesus' ministry in some of them, it is paramount to understand God's plans for them as well as the appropriate conduct and posture to not just enter the room but to remain in the room for the duration set by God.

Our lives are marked by a plethora of interactions with people, places, philosophies,

ethos, and things: in- person or digitally. The
twenty-first century has paved the way for
technological advances that have bridged the
gap among cultures, businesses, governments,
and systems worldwide. Meetings and
negotiations among business moguls and
entrepreneurs can take place via online rooms.
Digital and media applications such as Zoom,
Facebook, Instagram, Restream, and
YouTube have made meetings, classes, and
the exchange of information so much easier
among people all over the world.

Similarly, God facilitates the
transmission of His will, power, glory, tangible
presence, and so much more. This is not only

when we meet in rooms in person, but
through online gatherings as well. Jesus came
and died for us so that we can step out of
"church rooms" and step into other rooms in
various spheres of society with the message of
the Kingdom.

God wants us to remain open,
discerning, and willing to receive His pour in
designated rooms for the purposes of
releasing healing, revelation, teaching, training,
miracles, prophetic release, apostolic
impartation, and salvation. As the prophet
Isaiah stated in Isaiah 43:19 NLT *"For I am*
about to do something new. See, I have already begun!
Do you not see it?" It is God's desire for us to

know His perfect will for our lives (Romans 12:2) as well as move in His purpose daily.

This requires us to pay attention to the promptings of His Spirit as we enter a space (room) at the supermarket, the drugstore, the car dealership, the nail salon, and interact with others online. Four questions in entering rooms locally, globally, or digitally should be:

1. Do I belong in this room?
2. What is the lesson in this room?
3. Who do you want me to bless in this room?
4. Whom have you assigned to teach/train me in this room?

As you move forward in being prepared to enter new rooms, may the Holy Spirit guide you and lead you. *"I will instruct thee and teach thee in the way which thou shalt go: I will guide thee with mine eye." – Psalm 32:8*

CHAPTER 2

RIGHT PLACE, RIGHT TIME

For many years, I have been perplexed about the mystery of timing and proper location (place). Growing up in Port-Au-Prince, Haiti, I have been blessed by parents who know the LORD but understood the duality of time and place.

My father, Jean Hermann Manoly, is the fourth of five children and a first-generation preacher's kid (PK). He grew up in a Christian home with a father and mother who taught him and his siblings how to honor the LORD from a young age. A powerful Evangelist and Teacher, my father was the first one to teach my sisters and I how to love and value the Word of God. His righteous lifestyle from a very young age and zeal for the LORD have inspired and prepared me to walk into major rooms locally and globally.

My mother, Marie Christine Bruno Manoly, is a musician (singer and choir director) and an accountant who has a passion for traveling the world and enjoying the finest things in life. A humble yet wise woman, my mom (also a first-generation PK), has taught me the value of etiquette, possessing wisdom, as well as being prepared to make your mark in and out of the rooms where God leads me.

Both my parents have always raised the standard in our home and expected my sisters and I to excel in academics, music, career, society, church, and the world at-large. Growing up in a loving, yet structured environment with parents who understood the value of preparing the next generation of leaders truly helped me to better grasp the process that is necessary to steward the room well.

My parents have sacrificed a lot to allow my sisters and I to access rooms connected to superior education that granted us access to divine connections as well as preparation to enter greater rooms later. I am eternally thankful to God for blessing me with spirit-filled parents who live godly lives, honor God, believe in me, understand my calling, and inspire me to be everything that God has created me to be. What they have both prophesied over my life in academia, the marketplace, and the church have come to pass by God's grace. I am so honored to continue their legacy in the earth through my future children.

As a teenager and a young adult, I have often observed how some people who

have great connections and money were not
able to access certain rooms because of their
lack of preparation, character, etiquette, and
understanding of the opportunity extended to
them. Likewise, I have seen people who did
not possess great financial wealth or
connections get access to rooms that only
God could have made happen for them. Due
to being misunderstood as a child with
musical and creative gifts, I often would sit
back and observed the behaviors of others. I
thought that it pertained to a calling in
psychology; but later, the Holy Spirit revealed
that it was a part of the prophetic grace and
the preparation necessary to enter new rooms
and to represent Him well there.

The story of Esther in scripture is about being in the right place at the right time. She was an orphan whom God, through the counsel of Mordecai, granted access to the inner room of the palace to meet the king. However, she had to submit to the rigorous preparation required of all the young maidens who were also chosen to meet the king (Esther 2:12).

Due to her honoring Mordecai and following the recommendations of the eunuch assigned to her, Esther was positioned to have the ear and delight of the king, which caused her to be chosen as the new queen to replace Vashti. Once she became queen, Esther's true calling emerged out of a time of national crisis when her people were in danger of being destroyed. As an influential woman who was led by her mentor Mordecai, Esther rose to the occasion and went to the Throne Room in prayer as she mobilized all the Jews and her servants to join her in fervent intercession for God's favor (Esther 3:15-16).

Some of us like Esther may be in a holding pattern led by the LORD to perfect us in time while we are in the right place. Others may experience a longer process of being vetted by God so that we may access new rooms with godly wisdom and understanding as well as a humble and forgiving heart.

Esther rose to the occasion and risked her life as she entered "the room" where the king was located, and God spared her life as well as the lives of her people! King Ahasuerus extended his scepter towards Esther and allowed her to present her petition (Esther 5:2). She understood the assignment in the "prayer room" during her time of fasting which enabled her to walk boldly and confidently into the room of the palace where the king was to shift the destiny of a nation.

Joseph, the eleventh son of Jacob, was sold into slavery by his brothers who despised him (Genesis 37:28). He ended up at Potiphar's house as a slave and became the manager of his master's household. The timing for Joseph to serve Potiphar and his household was right but the place of his fulfilled promise was wrong. Potiphar's house only served as a training ground for greater. Once his training was over, God allowed Potiphar's wife to lie on him, which caused Joseph to be incarcerated in the prison located inside the palace (Genesis 39:20).

Unbeknownst to Joseph, the jail cell was the bridge to his promotion. God hid it from him because he was at the right place but had not arrived to God's time.

Nevertheless, God unlocked a gift within Joseph that was dormant: the ability to interpret dreams as well as the gifts of wisdom, knowledge, and prophecy. Crises, disappointments, and God-ordained detours have often been used by God to heal us of old wounds, take us deeper in trusting Him as our only Source, and to learn to forgive those who have deeply hurt us. Joseph was finally at the right place, at the right time, after being further stretched, healed, and developed by God.

It is vital to add that being at the right place, at the right time does not signify that we get everything we want and that we won't face challenges. Au contraire, we must be open and willing to allow God to have His way in us totally to fully access rooms in our future that will bring Him glory and bring deliverance to others.

Are you in a place where you feel as if God has forgotten you? Are you frustrated because the prophetic words that you have received have not yet come to pass? Does it seem that others get blessed faster than you? Be encouraged: God is preparing you to represent Him well at the right place, at the right time. Joseph's faithfulness, purity, and commitment paid off almost thirteen years later, while in jail, because God remembered him and caused him to have access to the king of Egypt, Pharaoh (Genesis 41).

The Greek word *Kairos* denotes the appointed time of the LORD. It is a moment designed by God where people, time, place, and events line up together to fulfill God's purpose in the earth. The emphasis here is that God determines the timings and the seasons when specific people meet, events occur, and revival takes place in the earth. Jesus, the Chief Apostle of our souls, was always at the right place, at the right time fulfilling His assignment in the earth. One of the parables used by Jesus during one of His teaching moments is the story of the ten virgins (Matthew 25:1-13). All ten virgins were at the right place at the beginning of the story. However, when the bridegroom arrived, only the five wise got access to the room while the five foolish were kept and missed the promise due to their lack of oil.

Another story in Scripture that has encouraged me greatly is that of Simeon, a devout and righteous man who prayed in the temple, awaiting the arrival of the Messiah as promised to him by God (Luke 2:25-26). Luke stated that at the appointed time, led by the

Holy Spirit to go to the Temple, Simeon saw Jesus with his earthly parents Joseph and Mary being presented; he prophesied to Mary about Jesus and his ministry as well as her destiny (Luke 2:27-35).

It is notable that Simeon obeyed the prompting and leading of the Holy Spirit in going to the Temple at a *Kairos* moment (a divinely appointed time) where the promise that God made to him came to pass, all because he was found at the right place, at the right time.

It is so vital that we do not just enter rooms because we desire to do so, but that we acquire what is necessary to remain in the room until the LORD blesses us to access greater rooms and places of influence. Preparation is essential to access God-appointed rooms where we will represent Him well and share the Gospel through the effective use of our gifts and talents. Later, I will address the heart posture and protocols of sustaining God's grace and favor in rooms.

May we be like the five wise virgins, with our lamps trimmed and full of oil, awaiting the arrival of the bridegroom! May we each remain in the process ordained by God to be trimmed (purged, cleansed, and cut) as in the story of Esther's and Josephs' preparation, and full of oil, a symbol of His anointing, full of the Holy Spirit. Yield to His process so that you may possess the fulfillment of His promises and prophetic words being at the right place, and the right time.

CHAPTER 3

UNRESTRAINED WORSHIP IN THE ROOM

In a previous chapter, I mentioned that rooms have specific purposes. Some rooms do not have as much movement in them as others. For instance, a storage room would not have as much traffic and events as a court room where cases are being evaluated frequently. The lack of event or movement does not diminish the value of the room. Inasmuch, when we think of worshipping God, most people think of a gathering in a church building or religious edifice. However, the scriptures are marked by individuals who broke the mold, refused to maintain the status quo, and by their unusual sacrifice and posture have shifted their legacies forever.

The scene recounted in the Gospels of Matthew, Mark, and Luke concerning the woman who broke the alabaster jar at Jesus' feet, offered us a great perspective as to the type of room that it was: as well as the main characters of the story. Jesus was invited to dine at Simon's house, as well as Lazarus (who was recently resurrected from the dead) and other guests (Matthew 26:7; Mark 14:3; Luke 7:37). The account of this same story in the Gospel of John stated that the dinner took place at Lazarus' house and identified the woman with the alabaster box as Mary, Lazarus', and Martha's sister (John 12:1-3).

This dinner took place in a room that was designed for members of the same household and/or guests to enjoy a good meal while having great conversation. What would have turned out to be an expected uneventful evening with Jesus (of course, Jesus would have shifted the atmosphere and brought healing or deliverance regardless) turned out to be a night that was recounted for generations.

While the men were reclining around the table at dinner, Mary (who was known as a

27

woman of ill-repute before getting delivered by Jesus) interrupted the dinner and showed up in the room with a very special assignment (Luke 7:37). I have read this story many times from my teens until this very day, and the question that always plagued me was: "how did Mary (the woman per the accounts of the Apostle Mark and Luke) access the Pharisee's house and the room where they were meeting with Jesus if she wasn't invited?" Perhaps, her brother Lazarus made way for her to access the room where Jesus was (John 12:1-3)?

Nevertheless, the important point in the story is that Mary interrupted the dinner on a quiet evening to pour out a very expensive perfume at the feet of Jesus. Many scholars and theologians have shared by the revelation of the Holy Spirit that the expensive perfume and her tears represented her unbridled worship to a King who would soon be beaten and crucified – Jesus the Messiah (Matthew 26:12; Mark 14:8; John 12:7). In the past two chapters, I shared that most rooms are designed for either business or work-related affairs to take place or for leisure.

Nonetheless, Mary understood the timing and place for her to release a costly gift and a major sacrifice to her Savior and her Rabbi who has healed her and taught her.

Jesus accepted her sacrifice and decreed that wherever the Gospel is being preached her story will be told (Matthew 26:13; Mark 14:9). She transformed a dining room into a worship room where she would express her gratitude to Jesus who changed her life. As a result of this, Jesus caused her to become famous!

Likewise, Jesus is calling each of us to follow the example of this woman who entered a room and altered her destiny forever by bringing with her the best gift that Jesus could ever receive: worship. The value of her gift was not how much the alabaster cost, but the courage that she had to overlook the ridicule of the people in the room who perhaps looked at her with disdain because they thought that she did not belong in the room with Jesus.

However, she was the only one who could discern what Jesus needed most at this strategic yet challenging hour approaching his greatest battle in the garden and his ultimate sacrifice on the cross (Matthew 26). Most of the guests including the host, Simon, viewed Jesus as a Teacher; yet she saw Him as King of kings and Savior of the world. Thus, she did not show up in the room with Jesus empty-handed. She brought two gifts: one to honor King Jesus (the alabaster perfume), and her worship/gratitude to honor the Savior who delivered her from her sins and demons. She was authentic and brought the gift of herself, a living sacrifice unto God (Romans 12:1).

As you spend time with the Holy Spirit in prayer, it is paramount that you ask Him what is the purpose of the room that you are currently in or are about to have access to: who or what is the assignment in the room? What is/are the lesson(s) to be learned? Do I bring a gift, if so, what does the host require or enjoy? How you view the room, grasp the magnitude of the assignment or divine connection, as well as your level of participation in the room will determine how well you steward the access given to you by God.

As a carrier of the Holy Spirit and the glory of God, it is vital that you remain ready to unleash the worshiper of Jesus in others as well as release your worship so that Jesus may enter the room to heal, set free, and deliver those who desperately need it. As the Apostle John stated in John 4:24: *"God is a Spirit: and they that worship him must worship him in spirit and in truth."* Worshipper of Jesus, arise, enter the room, full of worship, gratitude, and give yourself completely to Him. You shall shift the atmosphere in many rooms locally and internationally as you allow Jesus to step in the room through you. Show up, and let the Holy Spirit have his way!

CHAPTER 4

MIRACLES IN THE ROOM: THE PRESENCE AND MINISTRY OF JESUS

Various accounts in the Gospels of Matthew, Mark, Luke, and John have stated how Jesus transformed the lives of many people by entering rooms and by fulfilling His earthly assignment. One of the salient aspects of Jesus entering rooms is that He was confident in His identity and purpose. I have observed over the years that individuals who did not fully embrace their identity as sons of God as well as their God-ordained function and purpose as they access rooms often forfeit their mission and cause the window of opportunity to shut abruptly in their face, sadly never to be opened again. God desires for us to be wise and discerning as we enter rooms whether in the marketplace, at home, at work, at the city hall, in the courtroom, at the beauty parlor, at the barber, or the supermarket.

Jesus performed his first miracle at a wedding (John 2:1-11). He was in a room where the guests were celebrating the bride and groom. But His mother, Mary, asked Him to assist by providing the wine needed at the reception. Jesus explained to His mother that he may be at the right place, but the timing had not yet arrived (John 2:4). In the end, due to Mary's faith and His compassion, Jesus shifted the somber countenance of the bride and groom to a cheerful celebration with the latter wine tasting much better than the previously served wine (John 2:10). Jesus saved the day and redeemed this couple and their families from shame and disaster because He fully embraced His identity and purpose every day and everywhere that God sent Him.

The miracle of the paralyzed man carried by four men is noteworthy. Jesus was in a room teaching while four men interrupted him by bringing the paralyzed man through the roof (Mark 2:1-12). The faith, unity, and like-minded violent approach of the five men to getting to Jesus in the room were uncommon. One man received his healing and miracle because he and his friends were not afraid to disrupt the natural flow of events in a room where it is happening. Jesus applauded their faith and performed yet another great miracle. When faith is in the room where Jesus is miracles, signs, and wonders take place regularly.

Today, Jesus is looking for those who have bold faith and understand the Scripture that stated: *"...the Kingdom of heaven suffereth violence and the violent take it by force."* (Matthew 11:12 KJV).

Are you or your loved one in need of a breakthrough or a miracle? How desperate and creative are you like the paralyzed man and his friends to truly pursue Jesus' presence in the room where He is worshipped and reverenced? What do/would you allow to keep you from receiving your healing: pride, fear of being rejected or ridiculed, regrets and past disappointment, or the fear of failure?

Nothing stopped the four men from creating an opening (a room, an access point on a roof) to get the paralyzed man in front of Jesus so he could receive his healing.

Another powerful encounter in a room took place where Jesus healed a dead girl (Mark 5:37-43). Jairus, one of the prominent synagogue leaders, came to Jesus and pleaded with him to heal his sick daughter. However, the miracle was interrupted by the woman with the issue of blood (Mark 5:25-34). The faith of the woman with the issue of blood who pulled virtue from Jesus and became healed caused a delay in Jesus' arrival at Jairus' house. Nonetheless, the delay that frustrated Jairus and the others worked later in their favor because it was meant for a greater miracle to take place in a private room: raising Jairus' daughter from the dead.

Jesus only allowed his friends, Peter, James, and John to join him on this special assignment (Mark 5:37). This is noteworthy: we must be careful not to give access to everyone to the rooms where we assigned to be. Some with low faith, skepticism, carnality, religiosity, doubt, fear, and unbelief may inadvertently cause miracles to be delayed, and breakthrough to be hindered due to the lack of faith in the room. Thus, Jesus put out those who were crying and laughing at him but only allowed the child's parents and his disciples to be there in the room where the miracle would happen (Mark 5:40). The story in Mark concluded with Jesus raising the girl from the dead with authority (Mark 5:41-42).

As we move in and out of God-appointed

rooms, we must discern those assigned by the

enemy to stop us from fulfilling our godly

mandate. Like Jesus, we must be firm and not

fear the criticism of others but remain

intentional and focused on advancing God's

Kingdom in the earth at all costs.

It is vital for us to truly discern the

purpose and motive of the people that we

encounter in the rooms where God has given

us access to. Jesus was very keen in

immediately discerning who believed and who

didn't, who genuinely loved him and who

didn't, who remained connected to him for

the benefits that they received and who remained with him because they have been assigned and chosen by God.

As we move forward in accessing new rooms, we must do a faith check by asking the Holy Spirit to reveal to us who is in the room, what is their motive, who should be an ally in the assignment given to us, and who is assigned by the enemy to hinder us. Jeremiah 33:3 KJV stated*: "Call unto me, and I will answer thee, and show thee great and mighty things, which thou knowest not."* It is God's will to make known to us by His Spirit what He desires us to know. The Holy Spirit is the revealer of truth and of all things (John 16:13). May you continue to move forward in the rooms

ordained by God with the mantle, wisdom,

boldness, anointing, and faith of Jesus.

CHAPTER 5

THE UPPER ROOM: THE PRESENCE AND MINISTRY OF THE HOLY SPIRIT

Rooms are designed with short-term or long-term purpose. Those who plan it and have access to it fully grasp the intent of the leader. In past chapters, we have seen Jesus (who fully understood His purpose in the room), access much more than the original purpose of the room. We too must be careful that we do not operate from a traditional and religious mindset in accessing rooms where Jesus may want to bring healing, breakthrough, understanding, miracles, salvation, and strategies. We must remain ready, flexible, open, willing, full of faith, and swiftly obedient to execute our Master's purposes in the rooms where He sent us to represent Him.

After fulfilling His assignment in the earth and before returning to Heaven, Jesus gave His disciples the command of not leaving Jerusalem but to wait for the promise, the Holy Spirit, to come and baptize them (Acts 1:4). The simple yet profound command was diligently followed by His disciples with Peter as their leader. According to Jewish scholars, among those who have seen Him taken up to heaven about five hundred, only

one hundred and twenty met in the Upper
Room (Acts 1:15).

Acts 1:13 stated: *"And when they were
come in, they went up into an upper room, where
abode both Peter, and James, and John, and Andrew,
Philip, and Thomas, Bartholomew, and Matthew,
James the son of Alphaeus, and Simon Zelotes, and
Judas the brother of James."* The design and
purpose of the room were not mentioned in
Scripture. Nevertheless, God had already
prepared a place for them to gather until the
Holy Spirit came.

The mixed feelings of Jesus' disciples
in the Upper Room could be inferred as they

47

were mourning the departure of their Savior and Teacher, and perhaps felt anxious and uncertain as they prepare to embark on a new journey. Jesus' apostles, Mary, and the women, as well as Jesus' brothers were all present in the Upper Room awaiting the arrival of the Holy Spirit with great anticipation (Acts 1:14). Their obedience to Jesus' command to remain in Jerusalem and meet in the Upper Room was the catalyst to the birthing of the Church and a greater outpour of the Holy Spirit upon all flesh, a prophetic fulfillment to the prophecy of the Prophet Joel (Joel 2:28-29).

The natural and perhaps uncommon aspect of the Upper Room where they met was transformed by their unity and consistency in prayer, their faith and fervor to pray as they waited for the outpouring of the Holy Spirit. One of the major aspects of those who were in the Upper Room is their unity. "And when the day of Pentecost was fully come, they were all with one accord in one place." (Acts 2:1). The Upper Room was the place of preparation, transformation, and reformation where the Holy Spirit totally empowered them to be like Jesus in the earth.

In that room that may have looked so insignificant, the Holy Spirit came in suddenly like a mighty, rushing wind and with tongues of fire! (Acts 2:2-4). A life-changing encounter with the Holy Spirit in the Upper Room, being at the God-appointed place and at the God-appointed time, caused not just those who were there to receive power but to all those who would confess and receive Jesus as LORD.

The Church was birthed with the powerful and official entry of the Holy Spirit in the earth realm, the activator, the comforter, the helper, the teacher, and the revealer upon those who waited for him fervently in prayer. That same Spirit is available today to those who so desire to

receive Him in His fullness not just with the
evidence of speaking in tongues but to
prophesy (1 Corinthians 12:10) and to do
what pleases God (Philippians 2:13). The
Holy Spirit's assignment is to empower and
equip disciples of Jesus to walk with authority,
boldness, and faith to execute their callings in
the earth. His assignment is to testify about
Christ: *"...for the testimony of Jesus is the spirit of
prophecy." (Revelation 19:10b)*.

Without the power of the Holy Spirit,
you cannot fully operate at the optimum level
to fulfill your calling and destiny inside and
outside of the rooms where God has assigned
you to. Jesus expressly told His disciples:

"But ye shall receive power, after that the Holy Ghost is come upon you: and ye shall be witnesses unto me both in Jerusalem, and in all Judaea, and in Samaria, and unto the uttermost part of the earth." When a vessel carries the fullness of the Holy Spirit into a room, change, healing, breakthrough, miracles, answers, and so much more can happen.

It is important to emphasize that God's will is not for us to remain stagnant or locked in rooms. He desires for us to meet in rooms, like the apostles in Acts 1 and 2, to pray, study, worship, and to carry out the mandate given by Jesus in Matthew 28:19-20:

"Go ye therefore, and teach all nations, baptizing them in the name of the Father, and of the Son, and of the Holy Ghost: [20] Teaching them to observe all things whatsoever I have commanded you: and, lo, I am with you always, even unto the end of the world. Amen."

Likewise, when we meet every week at a particular location for worship, that sanctuary or edifice is not the only place where the Holy Spirit moves. As carriers of the Kingdom of God (Luke 17:21), anything miraculous and powerful can happen where ever we are sent to represent God. Congregations gather several times a week, not just to receive and go home with what was imparted in service, but to share what was received with a dying and hopeless world.

Our charge from Jesus is to impact our relatives, neighbors, communities, cities, states, nations, workplaces, governments, and every other sphere of society with the transformative power of the Gospel with the baptism of the Holy Spirit. Without the fire and power of the Holy Spirit, our well-meaning efforts will not yield God-intended purpose to bring salvation, healing, deliverance, and identity to the vessels who were chosen before the foundation of the world.

My pastor, Apostle G. Marie Carroll, has taught on numerous occasions that the Christian disciple and leader needs several "doses of the Holy Ghost", many impartations and fillings of the Holy Spirit to energize us, empower and equip us, bring us to the place of repentance and cleansing, purification and sanctification, as well as the willingness to embrace our calling and to exercise it in the earth with the utmost reverence and obedience unto God.

When Christian disciples and leaders make room for the Holy Spirit wherever they are meeting, regardless of the purpose and the room where they are assembled, He shows up (Matthew 18:20).

One of the first rooms that the Holy Spirit desires to take full control of is the room of our heart. Yielding to His leading and being willing to follow Him, makes us sons who have access to everything that our Heavenly Father has for us (Romans 8:14).

Invite the Holy Spirit today in the rooms of your life, the rooms of your home, businesses, workplace, church, and everywhere you go, and He will use you and transform the lives of those around you. Make room for the Holy Spirit today, and your life will be forever changed by the miracles that He makes happen just because you showed up in the room. So, go where God send you with the power and grace of the Holy Spirit, full of His fruit (Galatians 5:22-23) and His gifts (Ephesians 4:11; 1 Corinthians 12), and expect signs, wonders, miracles, and transformation to take place.

CHAPTER 6

POSTURE AND PROTOCOLS IN ROOMS

It should be considered an honor when God grants us access to rooms for His purpose. We must always remember that our accessing rooms are not for own agendas. We must ask the Holy Spirit intentionally what God's plan is for us in that room. Jeremiah 29:11 NLT stated: *"For I know the plans I have for you," says the LORD. "They are plans for good and not for disaster, to give you a future and a hope."* As we enter rooms we already have access to, as well as new rooms, it is paramount that we consult God's plan.

Proverbs 29:18 MSG stated: *"If people can't see what God is doing, they stumble all over themselves; But when they attend to what he reveals, they are most blessed."* Otherwise, although we may walk out closing great deals, signing important agreements, or other intended purpose, if we miss out on God's plan there, we have in a sense forfeited our assignment.

When we pay close to attention to the Holy Spirit's voice and follow His instructions when we enter rooms, great things take place. God wants us to always be ready to share with others the power of the Gospel, our testimony of being made whole and free, as well as provide opportunities where the Holy

Spirit intervenes with healing, salvation, teaching, miracles, and deliverance to those who are open and receptive.

Wisdom, Discernment, and Preparation

As I have stated earlier, when God grants us access to rooms, our first posture must be one of humility and a desire to learn the lessons He wants us to learn. If a vessel is overzealous and missed God's purpose in the room, he or she may go in thinking that what he or she brings to the table is the only reason why he or she has been given access to the room.

During my apostolic training, my Pastor and Mentor Apostle G. Marie Carroll allowed me to accompany her on several meetings nationally and internationally. As we entered these rooms, the Holy Spirit whispered to me, "Watch and pay attention to how your leader navigates the room. Be quiet, observe, and do what she does."

In some of the rooms, she observed and waited for the Holy Spirit to show her the reason why she was there beyond the actual purpose such as ministry, dinner engagement, or business meeting. In other instances, I watched God's wisdom operating in her when she would enter a "room" in a ministry setting by releasing the healing and power of the Holy Spirit flowing similarly as she would in her own church. During my training for ministry, Apostle G always told me: "Daughter, pray, study, and when you get there, discern the room. Be open to the Holy Spirit and follow His voice in real time." King Solomon stated in Proverbs 4:7: *"Wisdom is the principal thing; therefore get wisdom: and with all thy getting get understanding."* Godly wisdom is one of the greatest gifts that we can have. James 1:5 stated: *"If any of you lack wisdom, let him ask of God, that giveth to all men liberally, and upbraideth not; and it shall be given him."* Wisdom is the key that allows us to know when, how, and if we should even say or do anything at all when we enter rooms.

Added to wisdom, discernment is vital to us accessing rooms and maintaining the favor of God. According to Oxford Languages Online, discernment is defined as "the ability to judge well". Vocabulary.com defined discernment as "as a wise way of judging between things". Psalm 119:66 HCSB stated: *Teach me good judgment and discernment, for I rely on Your commands.* Discernment is not to be confused with the gift of discerning of spirits which enables the Christian believer to discern the presence and operation of evil spirits in people, places, and things (1 John

4:1; 1 Corinthians 12:10; 1 Thessalonians 5:21; Romans 12:2).

When we enter a room, we must first discern God's purpose for us being there: is it for teaching and training? Is it for divine connections? Is it for business only? Or is there a ministry assignment there? King Solomon stated in Proverbs 5:1-2 NLT: *"My son, pay attention to my wisdom; listen carefully to my wise counsel. Then you will show discernment, and your lips will express what you've learned.* It is God's desire for us to possess His wisdom and discernment prior to entering rooms. It is noteworthy to re-iterate that preparation is vital to the Christian vessel stewarding the room well and fulfilling the God-appointed assignment.

Unfortunately, over the past twenty-five years, I have witnessed extremely gifted vessels who refused to fully submit to the length and rigor of the preparation that God has appointed for them alone with Him and through His appointed godly Apostles, Prophets, Pastors, Teachers, Bishops, Elders, and Mentors. These vessels have unknowingly operated in pride, relying solely on their gift, and not trusting the LORD (Proverbs 3:5-6), and ended up with scandals, open rebuke, embezzlement, and so many other woes.

Moses submitted to God's preparation for forty years before he was sent back to the room where Pharaoh was on assignment to send God's people free (Acts 7:23). Let me be very careful to say that some of us have suffered a lot of attacks and humiliation for the cause of the Gospel. None of us are immune to errors and the temptations of the world. Yet, when we fully rely on God, and listen to His voice promptly, it would cause us to avoid further mistakes.

As an emerging and zealous Prophet twenty years ago, I have made mistakes in entering rooms thinking that I already possessed everything that I needed to succeed there. But God had to deal with pride, rejection, disobedience, vanity, bitterness, and rebellion within me before He could trust me to enter new rooms again. Through many years of breaking and purging, very difficult lessons and seasons, various sessions of biblical counseling, inner healing, and deliverance, the Holy Spirit has brought me to a sober place in Him where I realized that apart from Him, I can absolutely do nothing (John 15:5). Gifts alone will not sustain you in the rooms where God causes you to access. You must desire to be trained, prepared, vetted, and transformed by the Holy Spirit so that you can represent Him well in the room.

One of the greatest lessons that He taught me during my apostolic training is that a major part of the preparation for accessing rooms is that I must realize that I know nothing: it is more about unlearning first and being open to learn than coming in thinking that I already knew everything. Once I let go of what I knew that did not work or was not in Scripture, the Holy Spirit began to train me Himself and to appoint Pastors and Mentors over my life like Pastor Frantz David Eugene, Apostle Huberta Rejouis, Apostle Dr. G. Marie Carroll, Apostle Dr. McFarland Remy, and Reverend Deana Nail. Beloved, yield to God's preparation however He sees fit. Do not resist His breaking, the seasons of isolation and misunderstanding, being rejected

or overlooked during the process.

The Apostle Peter stated in 1 Peter

5:6: *"Humble yourselves therefore under the mighty*

hand of God, that he may exalt you in due time:"

Surrender fully, and like Joseph, when the

fullness of time has come, after you have

totally surrendered to His process and learned

the lessons well, God Himself will trust you to

go into rooms to say only what He tells you to

say, to do what He tells you to do, and to

demonstrate the Kingdom in its fullness for

His glory alone.

Honor the Leaders Who Gave You Access to the Room

Scripture is full of accounts of how God used His appointed leaders to make room for others. God used the high priest Eli to train Samuel in the service of the Temple and Samuel honored Eli (1 Samuel 3:1). Due to his obedience and honor to Eli, God appeared unto Samuel and revealed Himself to him in a life-changing way (1 Samuel 3:3-10). This encounter with God in the room where Samuel was sleeping catapulted him to his prophetic assignment. Yet, Eli although he was not wholeheartedly faithful unto the LORD, he was still used to train Samuel.

Submission to the authority placed over us is vital to us being prepared as well as stewarding the rooms that we have access to. Hebrews 13:17 expressed: *"Obey them that have the rule over you, and submit yourselves: for they watch for your souls, as they that must give account, that they may do it with joy, and not with grief: for that is unprofitable for you."*

Acts 10 gave us a powerful account of how God used a mighty Apostle to access a room where the Holy Spirit entered with unexpected demonstration. A devout centurion named Cornelius who loved God and gave to the poor (Acts 10:2) had a miraculous encounter with Peter, one of the greatest apostles. His faith in God and honor for who Peter was caused the Holy Spirit to fall fresh upon Cornelius' household and his guests while Peter was teaching (Acts 10:44).

This encounter did not just benefit Cornelius and his household but shifted Peter's ministry forever. God prepared the Apostle Peter for this unusual assignment to Gentiles through an open vision (Acts 10:9-16). There are times when God uses the room to sharpen His leaders while bringing salvation, healing, deliverance, and breakthrough to others who are hungry and seeking Him wholeheartedly. Again, sent vessels must discern God's intent for the room prior to entering the room through fasting and prayer, faithful study of His Word daily, as well as discern who's in the room, what they truly need, and how the Holy Spirit desires to orchestrate the miracle in the room.

Steward the Room Well

Accessing the room is much easier than staying in the room. It is vital that we steward the rooms that God gave us access to. Integrity, character, accountability, submission to God and authority are some of the necessary ingredients that assist the chosen vessel in maintaining God's purpose and assignment. To steward the room well, we must maintain covenant with those who open the room for us, our leaders, as well as our spirit-filled peers. They will keep us uplifted in prayer, give us godly wisdom, train us, and help us to avoid major pitfalls and the traps of the enemy.

Beloved, God is counting on you to represent Him well in the rooms that He is sending you to. Maintain the right posture, pure motives, discerning the God-ordained assignment, a pure heart, possessing the wisdom and discernment, as well as honoring God as well as the ones that He has ordained are vital to stewarding the room. Arise, beloved, and enter the room for the glory of

God!

CHAPTER 7

ACCESS YOUR GOD-ORDAINED ROOMS

PROPHETIC DECREES

Beloved, I decree and declare over you that you are chosen by God to enter rooms that will house His power and His glory.

This is your moment of preparation where God is intentional to train you so that you may abide in the Secret Place. I bless you to press into His presence and access The Throne Room perpetually.

This is your time of total reset and a moment of positioning for greater. Arise, son of God and go forth like Joseph to shift the economy of nations, peoples, and families.

Daughter of Zion, arise with boldness and submit to the Mordecai appointed by God to train and guide you for rooms of influence.

I decree and declare that you shall recognize your moment like Jesus and impact the lives of those assigned to you in the room.

This is your set time of grace, favor, overflow, and sudden promotion. As you show up in the next room, the LORD shall endow you with His wisdom, the understanding of times, knowledge, and discernment.

I decree that you are now embracing the assignment inside and outside the room. This is your time of being rewarded for trusting God during the moments of suffering for His glory.

Arise and steward the room well. As you walk into the rooms appointed by God, I decree that you are wise, discerning, understanding, and full of the Holy Spirit and power.

Yes, you are chosen to release worship, prayer, praise, the glory, sound teaching, miracles, healing, breakthrough, deliverance, and freedom in the room. Be bold, be present, be authentic, and take ownership of your God-ordained rooms!

You have been handpicked by God, trained, vetted, and are being sent forth with His power to shift the room and impact lives for His glory.

Walk in the room confidently, follow the Holy Spirit's leading in the room, be authentic in the room, honor your leaders who brought you in the room, and move with His grace in an out of the room effortlessly.

God has blessed you to move with power, grace, fire, and glory from the room to the four corners of the earth. Arise and access your God-ordained rooms now and change the world!

Greatness Beyond the Badge

The Three Key Principles for Self-Awareness

Michael Laidler

Softcover ISBN: 979-8-218-00618-1
Hardcover ISBN: 979-8-88759-124-7
Ebook ISBN: 979-8-218-00619-8

Download Your Free 5-Step Checklist Here:

https://greatness.michaelalaidler.com/checklist

Dedication

This book is dedicated to my mom, my sister and my son.

Quote

It is simple, create your legacy.

— Michael Laidler

Table of Contents

Introduction

The hardest part about determining who we are is determining who we are.

On June 17, 1994, the seeds of becoming a law enforcement officer were planted in me. It was a day that shaped my life. At the time, I did not realize how it would impact my life. On that day millions of viewers around the country were watching the infamous OJ Simpson car chase, including my family and me. The excitement, the thrill, and the idea he might not stop were exhilarating. I was only eight years old and did not realize that, one way or the other, he was going to be caught by the police. My family and I were glued to the television screen in anticipation of what was going to happen next. Once he was caught, the inevitable happened. He was set on trial for a double homicide, all types of people provided testimony, he provided testimony, the lawyer told the jurors about a pair of gloves at the crime scene and said, "If it doesn't fit, you must acquit," and eventually, he was acquitted." From

that moment forward, I aspired to be a law enforcement officer. Specifically, a homicide detective for the Los Angeles Police Department.

Eleven years later, I became a police officer for the Tallahassee Police Department, fulfilling what I thought was my destiny to be a law enforcement officer. In those eleven years, I didn't realize I never truly focused on who I wanted to be. I knew I wanted to have a badge but did not completely understand why. I only touched the surface of what drove me, what made me happy, and the career I wanted to be in.

For seventeen years, I have had an amazing career in law enforcement. I've developed relationships with a lot of good people. I've helped a lot of people. I've had the privilege of moving throughout several states in the country. However, there has always been something missing. I had the badge. The badge looked great and represented the highest level of honor to me. Yet, something was still missing. I knew something required more of my attention. I had a gap that made me feel like I was missing greatness.

For each of us, we have an opportunity to be great at many things. It took me years to realize that not only was I a law enforcement officer but I also had other characteristics and other traits that would be beneficial to me, my family, and anyone around me.

Essentially, I had never focused on self-awareness. I was raised by my mother and grandmother in Miami, Florida. My mother was a phone operator for Bell South,

and my grandmother, who was disabled, did not work a formal job. There was a lot of love in my house. On the flip side, there were no male role models and no one who had business acumen in our household. During my adolescent years and early into my adult life, I never had anyone help me work on my self-awareness. I never asked myself the questions:

- Who am I?
- Why am I here?
- What purpose do I have in this world?
- Whom can I impact?
- Where am I supposed to go next?
- How do I do it?

These are the types of questions I should have asked myself years ago but never realized how important it was to ask them.

In Tasha Eurich's book *Insight*, she and her team discovered only 15 percent of people are self-aware. The other 80–85 percent of people think they are self-aware. To be honest, I was one of those people in the 80–85 percent category. I never took the time to truly focus on myself and understand all the things that made me who I am today. It is tough not being self-aware. It is even tougher once you realize you are not self-aware and do not know how to find the answers.

In this book, I will provide you with strategies I have used to increase my self-awareness. It took me fifteen years of being in a high-stress law enforcement career,

where one's identity can easily be hidden behind a badge, to develop these strategies.

The answers in my life were never clear. It took time and effort and lost years to realize what I was missing.

I knew greatness was there. It was there for me. And it is there for you too.

In this book, we are going to take the journey together on a path to self-awareness. We are going to explore ways you can identify your own greatness.

Through my research and life experience, I've learned that three key principles help shape our self-awareness. The key principles are:

- The Discovery
- The Purpose
- The Path to Greatness

Key Principles

- 🔑 The Discovery
- 🔑 The Purpose
- 🔑 The Path to Greatness

From this point forward, you have a choice. You can choose to become more self-aware, or you can continue living your life wondering, "What is my greatness?"

If you choose to continue wondering "What is my greatness?" It is okay. Each person has to decide when they are ready. Some people realize they need to become self-aware today, while others are just not ready. The unfortunate side with the second choice is there are so many opportunities out there for you right now, and you will miss them because your self-awareness is low.

So I suggest you take the bull by the horns and start working on your self-awareness right now with me in this book. You have already decided to open this book up. You have chosen to begin to read it. You are already on the path to increasing your self-awareness. I'm optimistic that by the end of this book, you will be able to not only increase your self-awareness but also be more impactful to others around you and help them increase their ability to learn self-awareness as well.

It often helps to share your journey with others and to write out your thoughts. So at the end of each section, I have a reflection question with some hashtags. Share your experience because you never know who you might inspire, and include the hashtag so others can learn from your experience. You can also use the note pages at the end of each chapter to write down a few quick notes.

I look forward to walking alongside you on this road to greatness.

Key 1: The Discovery

"There are no secrets to success.
It is the result of preparation, hard work, and learning
from failure."

—Colin Powell

In 2007, I was a police officer for the Tallahassee Police Department. As a field training officer, I had an amazing squad. I was assigned to the swing shift, which worked from 4 p.m. to 2 a.m., on the south side of Tallahassee. The team, the agency, my life, and everything I could think of were on the right track. At the time, I was taking career opportunities as they came to me, so I did not discover some of the best opportunities available to me. One day, after a roll call, one of the captains pulled me to the side and asked me if I wanted to be in his unit. I never really considered being in that particular unit, but I figured I liked the duties they performed. I liked performing traffic stops and riding motorcycles, and the leather boots looked

cool. What's the worst that could happen? He told me that all I had to do was apply for the job, and it was mine. I applied and waited. A month or two passed, and when the selections came out, my name was not on the list. I was disappointed and surprised. I felt short changed on my career opportunity.

One day, not long after, a coworker told me she happened to be in earshot of the deciding conversation. This particular coworker was blunt. She did not hold back punches when she delivered any news to you. It was not because she wanted to hurt your feelings or make you look bad, but she wanted to let you know what you needed to fix. She told me that I had stopped trying and that I put in less effort when no one was watching. She said the person that was selected over me had increased his productivity and pushed harder than I did. I did not want to hear this from her. Unfortunately, she made an excellent point. She was 100 percent right about my performance. I reviewed my stats, and I realized my productivity had gone down in the past three months. I was not aware I had made it hard for him to select me for his unit. Essentially, I had placed myself in a losing situation.

This experience did not change my approach to how I operated. Rather, it impacted my next choice for my career because I thought I knew better. I was definitely wrong on that.

For years, I believed that situation was an unfair shot at my character. I believed it was not a true representation of the work I had previously put in, that it was, essentially,

a one-sided decision made by someone who did not know me. Since I was not happy with that outcome, I decided to look for new opportunities, a new career (border patrol), and a new place to live. That decision allowed me to justify not increasing my productivity.

Nowadays, a lot of people that I talk to have experienced similar outcomes. Their bad perceived experiences led them to leave a good situation, but then afterward, they realized they had not considered all the factors. It took me years to realize the error in my thinking.

Several questions and answers moved through my head that fueled my incorrect thinking:

- *Was it my fault? I doubt it. I did everything I could.*
- *Was it his fault? Definitely, he should have known more about me.*
- *Was it the agency's fault? Definitely, they should have asked more questions about me.*

Through my self-awareness journey, I learned a new question and answer to apply in such situations:

What should I have done differently to affect this decision? I should have taken a proactive approach to my personal growth.

The way you handle personal growth will vary. But since it is "personal" growth, you have the chance to dictate how you develop.

The main factor in all decisions about you is you. When you take a step back and look at everything that you have

been through and analyze all the factors, the common denominator is you. This is how self-awareness comes into play. It shows you what you are doing to contribute to the decisions that are made around you.

The journey to self-awareness is probably the hardest to start. It is hard for us to realize we are not self-aware. Even the most confident-looking person can lack self-awareness. The majority of us are stubborn and hardheaded. Stubbornness and being hardheaded are not specific to any one type of person. The downside to this is that whenever we hear something about ourselves that is upsetting, we turn off our ability to listen because we do not want to hear we are wrong about anything, and it hurts our feelings.

These hurt feelings come at an expense: your growth. I am not implying that what everyone says is true, but there may be some truths to what multiple people you trust say about you.

You have to discover what is true.

It is hard to start here. Nevertheless, you have to start somewhere. So, we will start in the discovery phase.

Reflection Question: Are you ready to discover what makes you who you are?

#thediscoveryphase #michaelalaidler

What to Expect in this Key

The Discovery

Wake-Up Calls (1 and 2)

Goals

The Mirror Methods

Failure

Wake-Up Calls

You probably picked up this book because you had a wake-up call and realized you need to discover your own greatness.

Often our path of discovery starts with big wake-up calls. Mine sure did.

Wake-Up Call # 1

"You are an underachiever."

Like most people, when you have a wake-up call, you do not really know that's what it is.

The beginning of my first wake-up call started in 2002. I was a junior in high school. I went to William H. Turner Technical High School in Miami, Florida. One of the things I recognized early in life was I wanted to be a police officer.

To continue my pursuit of being a police officer, I went to a technical school which focused on developing students for a career in the criminal justice system. Each school year, I learned more about criminal justice. It was a very

educational school. The school allowed me to take college courses during my junior and senior years, which gave me twenty-four credit hours toward a bachelor's degree and insight on what to expect during college classes.

I did pretty well in school and mostly received As and Bs. My Bs did not sit well with everyone. One day in my junior year, while I was in my criminal justice class, my teacher, who had already instructed me in my freshman and sophomore years, approached me while I was standing with a group of students. Mr. Williams was a college graduate of Florida A&M University. I never truly looked at him as a role model, not because he did not display role model traits but because I never had had a role model before, so I did not realize what his words were going to mean to me that day. I did not value the importance of mentorship.

When he approached me and the other students, he pulled me to the side. He said something to me that I remember to this day: "You are an underachiever."

Being sixteen years old and in my junior year, I did not know what that truly meant. I did not know what I did not know about myself or how I was handling my future. In 2002, when I heard those four words, the only thing I thought was, *What is this old man talking about*? In actuality, Mr. Williams was not that old and he knew what he was talking about. It took me years, nearly a decade, to truly appreciate the words he provided to me in 2002.

In 2011, another agent and I were patrolling a ranch road in Laredo, Texas, and the tire on our SUV went flat. It

was flat to the point that we could not drive it up to a paved road, so we had to stop where we were and change it. We jacked the SUV up and pulled out one tire. While putting the spare tire on the vehicle, the jack moved. BAM! The vehicle fell off the jack and landed on top of the tire and my hand. Luckily, the momentum from the vehicle hitting an inflated tire was enough for me to slide my hand out. However, the damage was done. By the time we finished putting the tire back on the vehicle and driving it to the nearest paved road, the top of my hand looked like it had a baseball underneath the skin.

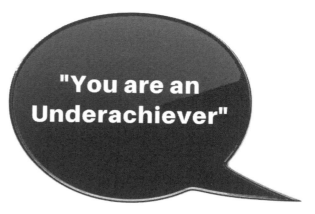

As I waited in the emergency room at the local hospital, these words entered my mind: *You are an underachiever.* My entire career in law enforcement flashed before my eyes. If I could not use my hand, I would not be able to handle a firearm. And if I could not use a firearm, I would lose the ability to work in the field as a law enforcement

officer. But since I had never really pushed myself to earn challenging promotions or embrace other law enforcement opportunities as they showed up, that was all I had. I saw opportunities to participate in other law enforcement activities, but I was not going after those opportunities for growth. I didn't do any long-term planning for my career. Instead, I just accepted what was given to me in my career. I was waiting for someone else to tell me what I needed to do. Simply, I did my job by coming to work each day, and that was all. But without the use of my hand, I might not have even been able to do that. I would be taken out of the field before I even had the chance to take advantage of everything it had to offer. Those thoughts were emotionally and mentally draining to my mindset. I did not understand Mr. Williams's words until that day.

As I waited there, I looked deeper at what Mr. Williams said to me. I realized he was telling me I was not doing enough. I was not fulfilling my potential. I was not going after goals that pushed me to my limits. I was taking life as it came to me. And it showed when I was in high school. It was always showing as an adult. Sure, I was doing okay, but I should have been doing amazing. I should have earned all As; I should have earned promotions in my job. He recognized it well before I recognized it.

In 2011, when I realized what those words meant, it sparked a desire in me to learn how to always do a little bit more. I did not have an immediate answer for what "more" meant, but I searched more often than I did in the past.

As I moved forward, I was always looking for ways I could be more and do more. One recent example of pushing myself to do more happened when I decided to write this book. Until I was twenty-six years old, I didn't read much. Although I had earned a college degree and I was working on a master's degree around that time, I only read books when I had to read them. I had no sense of urgency to read. I did not read newspapers. I did not read magazines. I did not read blogs. I was not into reading.

But to become an effective leader and an effective communicator, and to continue a mindset of learning, I had to read more. My desire and passion to learn more allowed me to slowly but surely increase my book reading. Now, whenever I glance at my bookshelf in my home office, I see that I have nearly a hundred books on it. For me to be writing a book was a complete change from who I used to be.

When you get a wake-up call like this, you realize how you have negatively impacted your life and more than likely the lives of those around you by being asleep to the ways you could be more and do more. You have to be able to take that experience and create a winning situation going forward.

Once I came to understand the truth of what Mr. Williams said to me, I reshaped my mind to push myself more in the areas of reading and listening to the advice of others. Ultimately, it provided the drive and motivation for me to write my book.

Reflection Question: What was your first wake-up call?

#wakeupcall #michaelalaidler

Wake-Up Call # 2

"I'm pregnant."

In 2012, I was living in Laredo, Texas, as a border patrol agent and a K-9 handler. I had everything a twenty-seven-year-old wanted in his career when it came to law enforcement. I had a great salary, amazing benefits, a work dog, and a take-home ride. I was healthy, and I was involved in numerous sports, including basketball, football, and softball. I was in a new house that I had just purchased in 2010 and had few expenses. Everything was smooth sailing.

On a Thursday in 2012, I had arrived home after several hours of playing flag football with my friends and coworkers. (As border patrol agents in Laredo, we had formed a strong bond. Specifically, the agents who liked to play sports. It was our way to relieve the stresses we faced as agents.)

It was a normal day for me.

When I walked into the house, I placed my gym bag in the office. I grabbed a bottle of Gatorade from the refrigerator and went back into the office to look at some fantasy football stats. I was hooked on sports.

My wife at the time yelled, "Michael, come upstairs." I did not think too much of it. I was used to being called by

her, like all happy couples. She was in the bathroom when I walked upstairs.

She said to me, "I'm pregnant."

I admit I was a little shocked, but I shouldn't have been.

We had already been trying for three years to have a child. We had tried several infertility treatments to have a child. For anyone using infertility treatments, I applaud you. It is a tough process. You have to be truly committed to it for it to work. When she told me that she was tired, I knew it was time to take a break.

After a few years of trying to conceive and her being ready for a break, we decided to slow down a little bit. We decided to see what God had in store for us. We realized we were trying to control conception. We figured when God was ready, we would be ready.

But my brain was not ready to hear those words.

Two feelings hit me all at once. I was excited and nervous. First, I was excited because one of the things I had been praying for finally happened. It was going to be my first child, and I felt like I was completely ready to have a child. Second, I was nervous because I quickly recognized that a lot of things in my life were going to change.

For starters, we had no family support nearby. Everyone I talked to and every book I read on parenting indicated it takes a village to raise a child. While we had established great friendships in the area, we knew that these friends would move away, and we would be required to raise this child without much support.

After "I'm pregnant," the next thing my wife said was, "We need to move back closer to family." Keep in mind that I had a lot of positives in my life. I had an amazing church home. In our marriage, we were operating on all cylinders. I was succeeding in my career. I could see and taste the next level of promotion, as I had stopped being an underachiever. I was in great shape. I was financially stable. I was moving in all of the right directions. I had a lot going for me, and it was not easy to give up all that I had worked for up to this point in my life.

But that was that, and we moved from Texas to Florida. In doing so, I discovered possessions and money are all temporary assets. Before leaving Texas, we had a combined income of $150,000. We were living high since our bills were minimal. When we moved back to Florida, I was making a base salary of $48,000 a year, she went to nursing school full-time, and we moved in with her

mother. Besides her parents and a small group of family members, we did not know anyone. We did not have a church home. We were starting over.

But all of those things did not matter because we were going back to Florida with our son.

I did not completely understand the magnitude of our decision to leave everything in Texas and move back to Florida. It was easy to see the things I was giving up. It was not easy to see the benefit I would gain from learning how to sacrifice for others.

When we sacrifice something, we do not always see immediate results. I know I did not see them in 2013 when I was driving my small family across five states to live with my in-laws. I did not see them when my bank account was seeing one-third of our previous income going into it. I did not see it when other people asked me if I was crazy for making a big move like that.

But little things happened over time which opened my eyes to the benefits of the sacrifice that I made. I was happier because my family bond was growing stronger. There is no replacing the ones we love. We were closer to family, and my son was able to experience his grandparents much more since we lived in Florida. I know I benefited from having my grandmother in my life. I wanted the same for my son.

The second area of improvement was my focus. I had to think about my personal growth. Back in 2012, everything was smooth. I was already on the track I had prepared for myself. In 2013, the track shifted and I had to

start at zero in my career. Starting over at zero after being so close to a promotion was challenging, but it increased my focus. I had to find different ways to grow myself and maximize my skill set. I had to grow to create a better environment for my family. And so I did. I built up my networking skills. A lot of people had great skills, but they lacked the ability to show others what they are capable of. They consistently undervalued networking and relevancy (I explain this in greater detail in the relevancy chapter). In order to grow, I couldn't undervalue meeting people and building relationships with them. I had to network and stay relevant.

The increased happiness in my family relationships and my increased focus helped me recognize what I was capable of. This new wake-up call forced me to take a hard look at myself, and I discovered there is more to life than possessions.

While giving up my great income and house (possessions) seemed like a step backward in life, it was actually a step forward because I was now focused on what mattered most: my family. And I pushed myself to advance quickly at this new police station, which brought me purpose.

Reflection Question: What possessions are you willing to give up to accomplish your life goal?

#lifegoals #michaelalaidler

NOTES

_____

_____

_____

_____

_____

_____

_____

_____

_____

_____

_____

_____

_____

_____

_____

_____

_____

_____

_____

_____

Goals

"Setting goals is the first step in turning the invisible into the visible."

—*Tony Robbins*

Wake-up calls will make you question what's next for you. I know each one has made me wonder how I am planning my future. They made me look at my life and determine where to go next to make improvements.

We all need to make improvements, but we can't make them all at once.We have to determine what we can do now and work from there. This is where goal-setting comes into play.

As I was rising through the ranks in the law enforcement industry, I didn't always know where I wanted to go. I did not know what my immediate or future goals truly were. As I started to discover who I was as a person, I realized I didn't have anything written down to help me focus on my destination.

I changed that and began making goals and writing them down. In my research on goal-setting methods, I learned about the SMART framework. Surprisingly, it was impactful right out of the gate. One of my goals was a speaking business. When using the SMART framework, I opened a business quicker than I thought I could. The SMART framework provides simple tools to complete your goals. I am a simple person by nature, so this framework was right up my alley.

I have one disclaimer for it. If you are not ready to build your self-awareness through the process of goal setting, do not use this system. It is meant for anyone who is serious about the growth process.

If you are past my small disclaimer (I am sure you are because you are reading this book), let's go over the SMART framework:

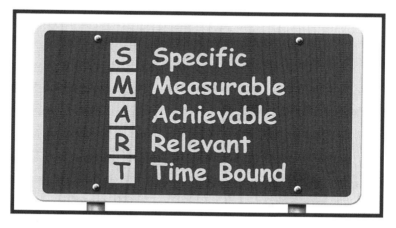

Specific: make sure your goals are narrow. When I say narrow, I mean specific to the point where no one—you or anyone else—can be unclear about what goal you are trying to achieve. For the sake of this framework, we will focus on earning a job promotion at your current organization. So to be specific, you would say, "I will earn a promotion in my organization." This example is very clear and does not include multiple goals. If I said, "I will earn a promotion in my organization, hire a new team member, and increase my social media marketing," it would be confusing. The SMART framework is designed to work one goal at a time; keep it that way.

Measurable: define the facts that prove you're making progress. Set a milestone to show what you have accomplished. For example, "I want to earn one promotion in my organization." The magic word in this example is one. Once you have earned one new promotion, you will have proof that you have passed this milestone. You can make the number variable based on the goal you are aiming for.

Achievable: you have to know what you need to fulfill this step. I would look at the credentials, experience, and skills required to earn the promotion. You could say, "I will take a leadership course in order to earn one promotion in my organization." When you look at this element, pay attention to everything you need to make it possible.

Relevant: verify that the goal aligns with your values. One of my values is financial independence. Early in my adulthood, I told myself I needed to create an

environment where my family could be financially successful at all times. As I planned future financial goals, I explored multiple ways to increase my income. All goals to do so aligned with my value of financial independence. If I earn it, I know what it will do for me and my family.

Time-bound: place a time limit on the goal. Whenever I have created a goal that did not have a time frame, I did not complete it. Everything and anything would come before the goal. Thus, I learned to establish exact time frames to ensure I finished my goal. For example, "In order to achieve my goal of financial independence, I will take a leadership course to earn one promotion in my organization in the next *six months*." If you do not complete this goal by the deadline, it gives you a chance to ask why it was not done.

There are goal-setting programs that talk about setting three-, five-, and ten-year goals. While these goals are very good for long-term planning, they leave out what happens in the interim. The long-term goal planning does not provide immediate results and it can make a person feel like there is no finish line. When I provide executive coaching, I start with three-month, six-month, and one-year goals. I make sure my clients understand they can achieve goals at a faster pace.

As I mentioned earlier in this chapter, when we utilize the SMART framework, we reach our goals quicker. If we were working towards a three-year goal right now, there is a good chance it could be accomplished in one year by using the SMART framework. If we work toward a one-

year goal, it could be accomplished in six months or less. I have consistently been amazed how I have surpassed my goals in less time than originally expected. Most of the goals we have are within our reach, especially when we put the time and effort into implementing them.

Any goal you choose can and should be placed in the SMART framework. Let's take it a step further. It is entirely up to you which goal you work on. For the sake of this book, it should be a goal which relates to your self-awareness. As you read further into the book, you will find different topics you can base your self-awareness goals on. Remember, the goal of this book is to build your self-awareness right away. The sooner you establish a goal for self-awareness, the quicker you can work on it.

Reflection Question: What is your one SMART goal you can start today?

#smartgoal #michaelalaidler

NOTES

The Mirror Methods

"The world is a great mirror.
It reflects back to you what you are."

—*Thomas Dreier*

Mirrors are undervalued. Most of us look into mirrors to brush our teeth, groom, put on makeup, or see if that car is riding our bumper. Over the last two years, I found a different way to use a mirror to my advantage.

A mirror or our phone (which can act like a mirror) helps us with self-awareness and goal setting.

How? We glance in a mirror multiple times a day, so it is a great place to put reminders. After making goals (which we discussed in the last chapter), we need to actually remember them. I learned a useful technique for remembering goals called the sticky note method. In David Goggins's book *Can't Hurt Me*, he talks about the sticky note method more in depth.

It's really easy. You take a sticky note and you write one goal on it. If you have multiple goals, you use multiple

sticky notes, then place each sticky on your bathroom mirror. As you complete the goals, you remove them from your mirror and place a new goal on there.

To be realistic, these goals cannot be extremely long, given the size of a sticky note. You have to be concise. They are quick reminders for different tasks, goals, and strategies we want to use to become who we can be and accomplish what we set out to do. The sticky notes allow us to see our goals before we go to bed at night, while we are performing nightly bathroom routines (brushing our teeth, taking out our contacts, etc.), and when we wake up the next day to do our morning routine. The sticky notes are constant reminders of what we want out of ourselves.

The second useful technique I have learned is to use your phone to remind you of your goals. Take a picture of your sticky notes, or a screenshot of a goals list you've made on your phone, and set it as your lock screen photo. (You can google instructions for how to do this on your specific phone.) This way, you can review your goals every time you pick up your phone. It is a quick way to reinforce what you are trying to achieve.

The third useful technique I teach people at conferences involves either your mirror or phone camera in selfie mode. I call it the selfie-mirror method.

I want you to do this exercise with me. With the selfie mode activated on your smartphone camera, repeat after me: "My name is [insert your first and last name]."

At conferences and events, I usually get a small chuckle the first time we perform this exercise. Since I say my

name—Michael Laidler—I can usually hear a few people say, "My name is Michael Laidler" as well. Hopefully, you said your name instead of mine. If you didn't, it is okay. You can do this exercise again.

I want you to notice as you do this exercise how I structure my name. I do not say "My name is Executive Director Michael Laidler" or "Lieutenant Michael Laidler." I start and end with my name.

Selfie-Mirror Method

Steps:

1. Activate selfie mode on your smart phone
2. Say - My name is [insert your first and last name].
3. Repeat until you can easily say your name before any professional title.

When it comes to self-awareness, a lot of us tend to forget who we really are.

Too many people feel their title is who they are. This is far from the truth. Outside of your company, no one knows your title. I constantly tell people, "No one cares at Walmart or Sam's Club if you are a chief of police or a warden. They only want you to pay for your groceries and leave." If you left your career today, they would replace you.

Now, it is acceptable to say "My name is Michael Laidler, executive director," or "My name is Michael Laidler, lieutenant." However, saying a title *before* your name takes away who you are, your true identity.

At conferences, I will introduce myself as "Michael Laidler, leadership strategist" or "Michael Laidler, professional speaker." I never say it in the reverse. It took me a while to realize the effect it had on my mindset. When I was placing the company's title before my name, I was losing a piece of myself. It was not what I meant, but it was how I believed I had to identify myself. I did not realize it was taking away from my self-identity.

I want you to establish who you are. It is fundamental to everything else we do going forward. A major factor in self-awareness is the *self* part.

I want you to get comfortable forgetting about your title and only using your name when you introduce yourself to others. You are more than a title. You are an individual who deserves to be recognized for who you are.

As you continuously do these exercises throughout the day, in the morning, at night, or at any point where you feel as if self-assurance is needed in confirming your identity, your mind will grow. The one thing that separates us from other species is our mind. What lies between our ears is a gold mine. We have to take each opportunity we have to grow it, as it helps us understand more of who we are and the goal that we are attempting to achieve.

For the next thirty days, I want you to try one of these mirror exercises. After doing this for thirty days, I want

you to go online and post how you feel. Did you meet your goals? It is OK if you haven't fully met them yet, because remember we are in the discovery phase, but did the sticky notes help you to remember?

Reflection Question: What did you discover about yourself as you worked toward your goals? What did you discover about yourself as you said your name out loud?

Reflection Question: Do you feel comfortable saying your name out loud?

Reflection Question: Do you feel you are taking more ownership of who you are?

#theselfiemirrorconcept #michaelalaidler

NOTES

Failure

"I have missed more than 9,000 shots in my career. I have lost almost 300 games. On twenty-six occasions I have been entrusted to take the game winning shot, and I missed. I have failed over and over and over again in my life. And that is why I succeed."

—*Michael Jordan*

In 2019, after being married for ten years, I got a divorce. I did not want to be divorced. I did not enter marriage believing divorce would ever be on the table. Unfortunately, this was the situation in June 2019. I was a divorced man who needed to continue with life.

While going through the divorce process, I discovered I could not control everything that happens in life. Of course, I wanted to control everything. I wanted to be the master of my destiny, but I could not be the master of this particular part of my destiny.

This was a pivotal moment in my life. I could choose to quit growing and blame the world, or I could sit down and figure out my faults. It was one of the biggest failures I had ever experienced, and I had a decision to make.

When failure and disappointment took over, my mind did not work as clearly, causing me to feel like a loser. But I had to sit back, decide how I was going to handle my response, and look at the reasons why this happened. I could have made many excuses, making it easy to deny what happened and become stagnant in my growth. Instead of taking this as a loss, I chose to take it as an impetus to succeed. I chose to win.

Winston Churchill said, "Success is not final, failure is not fatal: it is the courage to continue that counts." I had to find the courage to rise above the situation because I needed it for me, my son, and the rest of my family.

This time was important because it taught me something about myself that I never knew I had in me. I discovered I can take a failure and turn it into a positive outcome. But that did not happen overnight. It did not happen while I was directly in the storm. I had to fight through self-doubt and insecurity.

And most importantly, I had to take ownership and stop assigning blame. I learned that we all go through cycles of blame: blaming others, blaming yourself, denying blame, and accepting blame. It doesn't matter who you are. You are going to experience the cycles of blame. It is up to you how long you are in each cycle. It is up to you to recognize how to work through them.

Blame Cycle

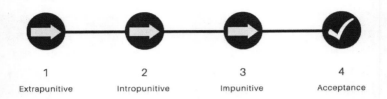

| 1 | 2 | 3 | 4 |
| Extrapunitive | Intropunitive | Impunitive | Acceptance |

The first cycle is extrapunitive or blaming others. When you blame others, you believe you were unfairly blamed and are too defensive to learn from feedback; you are full of excuses.

This is the cycle I found myself in at the beginning. I was blaming everyone else for what was going on with my marital relationship. I did not want to accept that I had anything to do with it. This was the easiest phase because I took no ownership of it. Excuses ruled this cycle for me. I had an excuse for everything. I had an excuse for why she was unhappy. I had an excuse for why things were not working out. I had an excuse for why I did not need to change anything about myself. It was much easier to point the finger at someone else than to accept areas I needed to improve on.

The second cycle is intropunitive, or blame yourself. When you blame yourself, you over criticize your errors, you do not make decisions because you are afraid of the results, and you accept too much blame to preserve a relationship.

This was my second cycle. I started to look at all of the things that went wrong and how I contributed to them. I had thoughts like, *I should not have said no*, *I should have been a better man*, *I can accept this issue because it was my fault.*

Fortunately, I did not sit in this phase extremely long. I have a strong personality. Because of this, I recognized that my contribution to the problem was only part of the situation.

Unfortunately, a lot of people suffer in this phase. When someone sits in this phase too long, you can become depressed and lose your sense of self-worth. You may even become suicidal. If you find yourself or someone you know in this phase and no recovery is imminent, I recommend seeking help immediately. If you have suicidal thoughts, call the National Suicide Lifeline at (800)273-8255 for free and confidential support. You may have an employees' assistance program available through your work. Some places specialize in suicidal ideations; you can find those through a Google search. If you believe you are at that point, put this book down, go help yourself, and find a healthy solution. This book will be here when you get back.

The third cycle is impunitive, or denying blame. This is not the same as blaming others. When you deny blame, you become angry when blamed, distort information to avoid blame, and you seem not to care about blame. Essentially, you deny failure to the point where you make it seem like it never existed. If anyone talks about it, you pretend it's not even true. You think it will go away if you do not address it.

At times, I was a little nonchalant about the blame. I acted like I did not care. It was a defense mechanism used to avoid the truth. I tried not to mention it to anyone in order to avoid placing the blame on either of us. I did not want either of us to appear to be the issue.

The fourth cycle is accepting blame. This is usually the final phase when you understand you have to move on.

This was also the most relieving phase of them all. I did not solely blame her, I did not solely blame myself, nor did I deny that a failure had occurred. I accepted there was an issue and each of us had a role in it. During this phase, I worked on getting over the blame game. I worked on using this situation to my advantage.

Any failure we face can have benefits. We have to decide which factors will benefit us. During this failure for me, I grew a closer relationship with God and my son. I found myself spending multiple days in church and connecting more with others who believed in God. This time with God was not a time to speak about the pitfalls of divorce. It was a time devoted to focusing on the positives I had in my life. I learned to highlight my wins and not promote the losses.

I also found myself spending more one-on-one time with my son. I had to find more creative ways to make sure my time with my son was maximized. Sometimes it was spending all day doing what a four-year-old wanted to do. The other times included finding meaningful activities that would increase his enjoyment of life. Since I grew up with no father figure in my life, I wanted to have as much time with my son as I could. I made a focused effort to

spend time with him and made sure he understood how much I loved him.

So from my failure came growth. As you look back at your own failures, can you see any way you grew from them? If not, what can you do moving forward to grow from them?

If you are still stuck in the blame cycle, you will not be able to grow.

Many people fall into the cycles of extrapunitive, intropunitive, and impunitive. Although failure is inevitable, blame can be managed. When we allow ourselves to fall into these three categories, it can derail everything we have worked for. It is in your best interest to figure out which category you are in when you fail at anything in your life.

One of the strategies I find valuable in dealing with failure is taking different personality tests. Two of my favorite personality tests are the Myers-Briggs and the Big Five. Both of these personality tests can be located by doing a Google search and can be taken in a short period of time. They both provide insight into how you deal with failure. If neither of these tests fit what you are trying to discover about how to deal with failure, use the power of self-reflection.

As I have developed my self-awareness, I find myself continuously evaluating how past experiences have shaped my future. I also evaluate how I reacted during difficult times and what I would do differently today.

Back when I was a field training officer for the Tallahassee Police Department, I was the first person to provide feedback to new officers. This was exciting and stressful. If you have ever trained anyone one-on-one, you understand how tough it can be to provide feedback to someone you barely know, especially when the feedback can make the difference in their career.

One night, I found myself training a newer officer who had only been in the police department for two months. These two months included several weeks of high liability training, like firearms, defensive tactics, and driving skills. I was the second person to train this newer officer. After observing her on a few calls, it was time to let go of the reins and have her act on her own. She did well, and at the end of the call, it was time for feedback. I asked her, "How do you think you did?" My goal was to gauge her insight into her performance. She responded in a surprising manner. She initially outlined all of the negative things that happened on the call. She mentioned how she did not talk to the complainant right away. She pointed out how she did not pat search the suspect before she spoke with him. As she was explaining how she performed, I recognized she was becoming more disappointed with herself. She didn't mention any positive actions. I had to bring up how she identified everyone in the beginning of the call and separated them. I told her that she interviewed everyone with very good details and made the right call at the end. Her disappointment turned into satisfaction.

At that moment, I felt like a failure when she had listed all her own failures. After engaging in some self-reflection, I discovered what I had learned from that failure. I realized her reactions were based on my training. I did not know I had to train someone on how to accept and learn from failure and highlight their success. I did not know how to build someone up. When I went on to train other people, I taught them this skill. At some point, we will all fail and enter the cycles of blame. But by discovering what cycle of blame we are in and moving through it, taking personality tests like the ones I mentioned in this chapter, and making time for reflection, we can alter the way we respond to failure. In this discovery phase, you need to determine where you are at. Are you currently stuck in a cycle of blame? Are you past the cycle of blame but still stuck because you haven't learned from a past failure? Or have you learned from a past failure but just need to self-reflect to see what you learned?

We cannot hide from failure because it will happen no matter what we do. All we can do is be prepared when it happens. It will never be fun, but we can be ready for it.

If you still need help responding to failure, reread this chapter. Try to determine what cycle you are in and how to get past it. The quicker you get to accepting blame for a failure and continuing with your life, the faster you will be able to get back to increasing your personal growth. I believe you can respond more effectively to any failure when you know how to work through the cycles of blame.

How we deal with failure is a big part in discovering who we are.

Reflection Question: What failure have you experienced in the last few days? What lesson have you learned from it?

#failure #failuretosuccess #michaelalaidler

Key Points for Self-Awareness

★ There is more to life than possessions or tangible items.

★ Look back at your wake-up calls to determine what you need to improve.

★ Make clear goals for improvement.

★ Use the mirror method to remind yourself of your goals and to embrace who you are.

★ Assess what you can learn from past failures to move forward.

NOTES

Key 2: The Purpose

"What you get by achieving your goals is not as important as what you become by achieving your goals."

—*Zig Ziglar*

I grew up in Miami, Florida. I was raised by my single mother and my grandmother. Early on, I realized how hard they worked to make a good life for us. They made every effort to make me and my sister happy. They sacrificed a lot for us, and they wanted us to know we came first to them.

Our neighborhood was filled with one-story single-family homes. Our mailbox was about five feet off the ground on a wooden pole with a chain-link fence underneath that had metal spikes on top. The top of the metal spikes almost touched the bottom of the mailbox. One thing I used to love as a kid was getting mail from the mailbox. It made me feel important that I could contribute something to the household. I would run out

to the mailbox after I saw the mail carrier leave, climb the fence, get the mail, and take it back into the house for my grandmother to read.

One sunny day, I did my normal routine of running out and climbing the fence to get the mail out of the box. As I hurried up the fence, my foot slipped. Instead of falling, I was suspended in mid-air. I looked up and saw my left arm was caught on one of the metal spikes. The spike had punctured the interior part of my left bicep, and I was hanging on the fence. All I could do was hang there.

I called for help but got no answer. No one inside could hear me. The pain from the skin pulling away from my bicep was excruciating. After a few minutes of hanging there wondering if I would ever be free of the pain, I looked up and saw our neighbor John running over to me. His eyes were wide as he lifted me off the fence and took me inside. My grandmother was shocked. Immediately, she called the ambulance. A couple of hours later, I had fourteen stitches in my left bicep. But I kept retrieving the mail despite the potential for danger.

For me, retrieving the mail each day provided me with a chance to show my mother and my grandmother how I wanted to contribute to the household. It felt good to do something for my family. It felt good to have a clear purpose. To live out your purpose, you need to develop yourself.

When it comes to developing yourself, it's important to know why. Everyone's reason is unique to them.

Four ways have worked for me to help me develop myself and live out my purpose: having a unique selling position, minimizing dissonance, increasing my relevancy, and preparing for the next life cycle.

Reflection Question: What is your purpose for self-awareness?

#selfawareness #michaelalaidler

What to Expect in this Key

The Purpose

Unique Selling Position

Dissonance

Relevancy

Next Life Cycle

Unique Selling Position

*"Your brand is what other people say about you
when you're not in the room."*

—*Jeff Bezos*

This book is not about personal branding. It is not a book to increase marketing sales for business nor is it a book about social media. But a unique selling position doesn't just relate to branding and marketing. It can help with defining your purpose, which helps you achieve greatness.

In the beginning phase of starting my own business back in 2017 as a professional speaker and leadership trainer, I never really considered what made me unique as a person. I had worked for three law enforcement agencies in multiple states. I had worked in all types of positions during my career. But I was never trained by any of these organizations on how to make myself stand out.

One thing I learned when I started my business was I had to take control of how people viewed me. When there

are thousands and thousands of businesses out there, you have to find a way to improve your skill set. You have to find a way to stand out in the crowd.

The first step is defining where you want to go. If you do not have a destination, you cannot ask anyone to follow you. Without knowing where you want to go (your purpose), you will not know where to focus your energy. I became a professional speaker in 2017, but it did not happen overnight. However, because I knew this is where I wanted to go, I put in the effort to make it happen.

To do this, I knew I had to get better at speaking. I grew up with a stuttering issue. I did not stutter because I did not know what I wanted to say; I stuttered because I had so much to say, I wanted to say it all at once. I had to work to overcome this impediment. Although it is something I still struggle with, I have improved my control over my speech remarkably, and I do not allow it to prevent me from doing what I want to do.

You can always improve with additional training. So I dove into training to improve a few areas like the timing of my presentation, the use of filler words, and pausing as I spoke. During each Toastmasters meeting, a designated evaluator helps the speakers develop their skills. The evaluator provided positive feedback on the meeting, the presentation, and the team members and gave tools on how the speaker could improve. I performed this role as much as I could. I wanted to learn how to give and receive evaluations. As the evaluator, I listened more closely to the nuances of a speech, which helped me improve my skills.

When one sits down and provides you with an evaluation on how you did, it is hard to understand what you did right and what you need to improve on. If a speaker does not seek out evaluation of their performance, they are short-changing themselves and their ability to make high-quality presentations.

My speaking abilities did not improve overnight. I had to endure a lot of evaluations to grow. They were not always pleasant, but they were always informational. I took a little bit from each one to improve on future presentations. To ensure I increased my speaking skills with the help of evaluations, I made over fifty evaluated presentations over a four-year span in Toastmasters. I would not have been so committed had I not first defined my destination.

My purpose defined my destination. I realized quickly how becoming a better speaker would ultimately lead me to be a stronger communicator. I knew I had to know where I was going before I could push myself to that level. If not, I would have been swinging in the dark and unable to direct my purpose on a focused path.

The next step is to leverage what makes you different. When it comes down to it, we all offer something different. This is something we can use to our advantage. You have to emphasize something about you that people will remember. Robert Reich, a former US Secretary of Labor, did this by opening every speech with a joke about his short stature. At 4'11" this was something that made him different, and he used it to his advantage.

You may not always see it, but being different is part of your purpose. As you grow and understand more about yourself, you will see that you may not be the smartest, fastest, strongest, or richest around town. However, your difference is your strength. It is a strength no one else has but you. You will be able to use it to enhance your purpose in your life, as it allows you to concentrate on what makes you unique. You can spend more time on developing yourself as you recognize these differences.

Let's take a quick look at what makes each of us different. Think about five characteristics you believe are unique about yourself.

1. _____
2. _____
3. _____
4. _____
5. _____

Do not overthink these characteristics. These characteristics are for you.

Now, take the first characteristic you wrote down. Over the next three days, take fifteen minutes a day to conduct research on it. Keep it simple. Type the characteristic into Google and see what comes up. The positive, different things you learn about this characteristic will give you ways to stand out.

For example, I am ethnically diverse. I am a mixture of African American, Hispanic, and Caucasian. Due to this mixture, I have found myself being able to adapt to

various groups of people because I have been immersed in all three cultures. It took me years to appreciate this characteristic. After I took the time to research it, I could better understand the people around me since it required me to take deeper looks into different cultures. I know more about other cultures than I would have ever imagined. I would not have ever learned their unique differences if I did not see how my ethnic diversity was a unique characteristic for me.

The third step is to learn to better control your attitude and appearance. These two things convey how you arrived at your destination. They illustrate your story to others.

At an early age, I worked on my attitude to manage the way I responded to people and things I could not control. It was not fun, but it allowed me to minimize my stress. It is always up to you how you respond to people. If someone treats you poorly, you can take two approaches: you can be vengeful and try to make them feel little, or you can try to understand the situation and respond as the bigger person. It is not easy, but it is definitely doable.

Just like with our attitude, we can always control our appearance. I know when I dress a certain way, it makes me think in a certain way. I do not know if there is a science behind it. I just know it works for me, and I feel better when doing it. This does not mean that I dress in $2,000 suits. It just means that I have a clean appearance, I iron my clothes, shave my face, and clean any scuffs off my shoes. When I look good, my mind works more fluidly.

Both of these aspects of life, attitude and appearance, allow me to move forward and continue to grow. When we do not control our attitude and our appearance, we lose our ability to focus on our own story and on our own purpose. When managed correctly, they will allow you to navigate more effectively during tough times. Don't allow a lack of attention to these two aspects hinder your ability to tell the rest of the world how great you are.

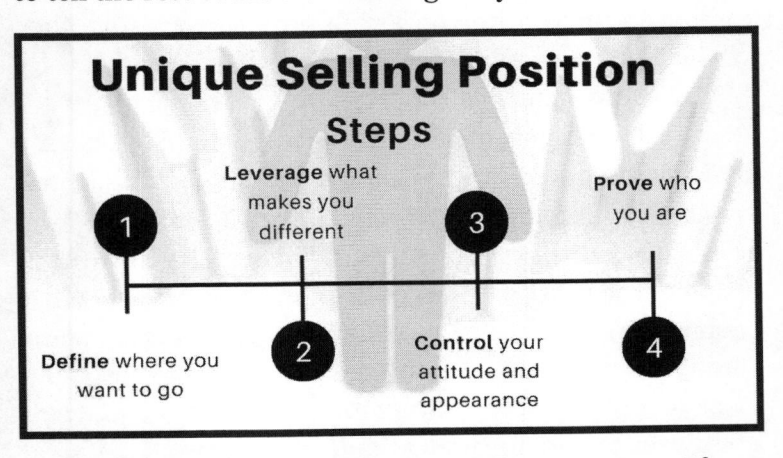

The final step is to prove who you are. If you spend all of this time defining who you are, leveraging what makes you different, and improving on aspects of your life but you do not tell anybody, then how will they know?

When I do mentoring, I talk about networking. After you develop your skill set, you have to promote yourself in a manner where people will be able to see you. You might know you are good, but who sees it?

I am not suggesting you go and brag about how good you are, but you do need to get noticed. Do not go around saying, "Look at me," "I am about the best around here," or "No one else can do the job the same way I can." Rather, find those natural moments when you are in the same room as the people who can teach you how to be a better version of yourself. I explain more about this in the relevancy chapter.

As you prove who you are to others, over time, they will help you on your path to greater self-awareness.

Does that sound weird?

It seemed weird to me at first, too. I thought by proving my worth to others, I was doing something wrong. It felt strange and unnatural.

That is far from the truth. I have benefited greatly from people knowing I am a professional speaker, especially people who knew me before I started my speaking business. Family, friends, and acquaintances continue to reach out to me to find ways to be part of my self-awareness journey. They want to help me understand my purpose. They want to provide me with positive affirmations and connections to other like-minded people. They want to see me succeed. All of that comes from not hiding my intentions of building my purpose through my unique selling position.

As you continue to build your unique selling position, you have to stay consistent and committed to yourself. It is going to take time to build people's awareness of you. This is no easy feat. But it is a worthy goal.

Reflection Question: What are you doing to develop your unique selling position that defines your purpose and establishes why you are improving yourself?

#iamunique #michaelalaidler

NOTES

_____

_____

_____

_____

_____

_____

_____

_____

_____

_____

_____

_____

_____

_____

_____

_____

_____

_____

_____

_____

_____

Relevancy

"*Stopping advertising to save money is like stopping your watch to save time.*"

—*Henry Ford*

As police officers, a part of our purpose is in our job. We make a difference in the lives of others. Serving the community gives us purpose. But in order to fully live out that purpose, we need to make ourselves relevant at work.

I didn't realize the importance of relevancy until about 2013. But once I did, I saw how much it impacts understanding my purpose and developing my self-awareness. It is hard to live out my purpose when I don't show my worth. Yes, you have to do this. You have to show your worth. It is a physical action that allows others to see where you are at and where you want to be (your purpose).

I was in my last semester of my MBA program at Morehead State University, and it was my first time taking a course on leadership.

During the semester, the professor emphasized that if nobody knows how good we are at completing a job, that is just a lost skill. I took his point of view very seriously and wondered how true it could be. I wanted to put his theory to the test since I was entering a new agency.

In 2013, I began to work as a correctional officer and participated in extracurricular activities after work. Some of these activities involved softball games, grilling food, and playing cards. My favorite activity was a card game called Spades. I had already been playing it for years. I took this particular skill set, if you want to call it that, and used it during these extracurricular activities at work. From playing Spades, I knew which hands were considered "winning hands." I knew how to work with a partner to win. I knew how to lose and not get upset by it. I then used these skill sets to connect with my teammates and overcome failure. In doing so, I showed others I had skills that were relevant to them.

Essentially, I increased my relevance at work. My coworkers and teammates saw me as a valuable player. I used these newly acquired skills to network with the decision-makers at my organization and find a connection with them, so I could showcase my professionalism and my passion for some of the activities I did at work. Now, this was not a time to brag, but it was a time to create relationships that may have not been established in other environments, especially during work hours.

Ways to Increase Relevancy

1. Increase your visibility with the decision-makers

2. Understand what people are looking for

3. Recognize how people feel when you ask them for help

4. Invest in a 360-degree assessment

This worked for me because I combined relevancy with my skill set. After a deeper dive into relevance, I looked at four areas where a person can increase their relevancy:

1. Increase your visibility with the decision-makers. Find a way to be around the decision-makers. If they are involved in March Madness, get in on the action. If they belong to a local kickball team, sign up. You can show them your skill sets outside of a work environment and help them see you offer something they need.

2. Understand what people are looking for. As you understand more about what they care about, you can look at your own value and what you bring to the table and ensure that it is highlighted when you are around them.

3. Recognize how people feel when you ask them for help. As a leader, it is always an honor for people

to ask for my help. I know when someone asks me for help, it means they appreciate my knowledge. Reach out for help and then thank whoever that person is for providing you with the help. You will be surprised how much they appreciate your confidence in them.

4. Invest in a 360-degree assessment to get feedback from people at every level of your organization and also evaluate yourself. These assessments help you understand your strengths and weaknesses as an individual. My friend and business partner, James Summers, professor at Iowa State University, demonstrated how important 360-degree assessments can be for leaders. He explained that the way people view themselves will differ from the way others view them. Whether it is good or bad, there is a difference. Once you know the difference, you have a starting point to improve on. This starting point helps you focus on who you are in the eyes of others. Once you grasp the view of others, you can use their perspective to make yourself better. Remember, the more viewpoints you have, the more you can see. As you learn these different areas, you recognize what will work and will not work when it comes to showcasing your relevancy to others. If you have not done one yet, go and get one.

No matter how you look at it, increasing and maintaining relevance is important. Your skill set being recognized by others is your capital. As they recognize it more, they will be more comfortable trusting you and assigning you important cases so you can fulfill a part of your purpose to better serve the community.

People are developing themselves each and every day to make themselves better than you. Take a quick minute or two and think about your competition. What are they doing to showcase their skills? Is there someone who is doing a little more than everyone else? They are promoting their skills to the people who can dictate your future. Do not allow your opportunity to slip by.

Reflection Question: What makes you relevant in your organization? What makes you stand out among your peers?

#relevancy #michaelalaidler

NOTES

_____

_____

_____

_____

_____

_____

_____

_____

_____

_____

_____

_____

_____

_____

_____

_____

_____

_____

_____

Dissonance

"Dissonance is the truth about harmony."

—*Theodor Adorno*

A 2013 study called "Life Expectancy in Police Officers: A Comparison with the U.S. General Population" by John M. Violanti[1] compared the life expectancy of white male officers in Buffalo, NY, to their peers outside of law enforcement. It showed that at all ages the life expectancy for those in the force was significantly lower. This is an important issue to look at. It's clear that something's not right here.

What causes the life expectancy to decrease for those in law enforcement?

Life expectancy is lower in these populations because of dissonance. For the objective of this book and our purpose, dissonance is when our beliefs and behaviors do not align, resulting in an inconsistency in what we say we want to do

---

1. John Violanti et al, "Life Expectancy in Police Officers: A Comparison with the U.S. General Population," *National Library of Medicine* 15, no.4 (2013): 217–28, https://www.ncbi.nlm.nih.gov/pmc/articles/PMC4734369/.

and what we are actually doing. On the surface, this may be something as little as being required to perform an activity you said you did not want to do but you did. It can mean making decisions for one area of your life but always looking at what you missed out on. Or you say you have a specific belief (e.g., believe strongly in the importance of family) but you behave contrary to that belief (e.g., you never see your family). There is a level of disharmony when dissonance is happening in our life. For those of us in law enforcement, it is a real issue because we strive to be great at what we do, yet focusing so much on our job causes us to not live out our beliefs and value system.

If we are to fully live out our purpose, we have to take the time to actually work on ourselves. Our job is not our full purpose. Sure, our job is important and allows us to contribute to our society, but we have to have more purpose than that.

Have you ever known someone who became the person their company wanted them to be and no longer seemed to have a mind of their own? Was their title more obvious than their first and last name?

How about a person who stays at work sixteen hours a day for five to six days a week?

Or—this is going to be a little bit more personal—have you ever thought about what separates you from your organization?

People falsely believe that the more time you spend at work, the more consistent results you have, and the more you are going to be appreciated.

When you lose yourself in your work, every part of your life will suffer. You enter into dissonance, and all of the results you initially had start to slowly fade away. One of the main reasons for lowered performance is you do not know who you are anymore; you are no longer living your purpose. It is not something you do purposely, but it happens over time when you continuously focus on everyone and everything but yourself. You may think your personal life is great, you may think you have a great relationship with your kids, and you may believe the relationships you have with your significant other and peers are solid. But all of that is superficial and temporary when you are in a level of dissonance.

The cost of sacrificing everything else over an extended period of time is that you lose yourself. And it's unfortunate because the people who we see as most successful are often ones that lose who they are and their purpose.

This worries me about individuals who spend a lot of time at their work or spend a long period of time in a high-stress environment. They end up with weaker mental and physical health because they never took the time to develop themselves. We all have felt the pressure to slow down, but we don't all take the time to do so and give ourselves the time that we deserve. One of the ways to reverse the cycle of dissonance is renewal, which we will talk about later in the book.

The quickest way to remedy dissonance is to realize that your organization will run with or without you. Most organizations were started before we joined and

will continue after we leave. This is particularly true in government agencies. We should always give our best to ourselves first and then to our work. If we are not operating at a high level, then we will never be able to give our all to the people we love or to our organization.

Most of us know inside that we need to do more with our own growth. We just find excuses not to. When I am pushing others to focus on themselves, I hear phrases like, "I am too busy to read," "I have to finish this project first," or "The phone does not stop ringing." All of these phrases place the organization before you, making the organization more important than your own well-being. Stop that now.

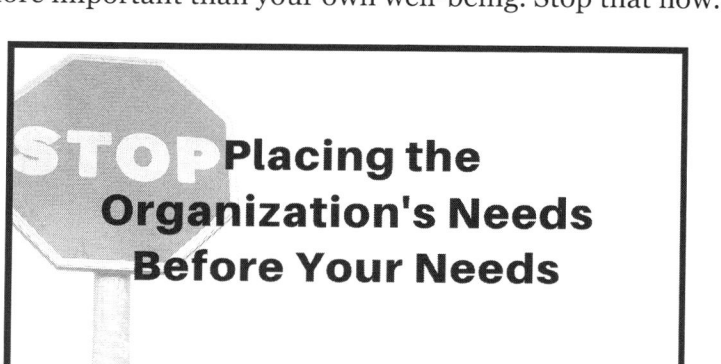

Although we can see the writing on the wall that something is wrong, success tricks us into ignoring reality, especially if our income is high or all our needs are being met on a continuous basis. We overlook when we have a bad day or things start to slip away. We find ourselves increasing our energy just to keep up with the success we previously had.

This then leaves us with little energy for ourselves, resulting in decision-making becoming harder and our confidence being lowered. I can remember times in my life when I was going so fast that I was slipping in places that I should have not slipped in. I was rushing decisions because I had to move on to the next project. I did not take time for myself, and the results were obvious. My ability to make decisions suffered. This was a pattern of dissonance.

As dissonance increases, our values and our beliefs go to the backburner, then our personal relationships suffer. I know we say it is lonely at the top. But this does not mean we cannot enjoy our time on top with others and build relationships. This saying does not mean we have to live a life by ourselves; it only means the decisions you have to make are not always agreed upon by everyone else. If we choose to be lonely, it is not because we are at the top. It is because we didn't take the time to nurture our relationships.

You cannot hide from dissonance. You cannot run from it like it is a scary movie. Denial is easy, but it is not right. But often, even if you do face it, you try to slap on a quick fix. You may think that taking a small vacation or having a few staycations are the key to getting out of dissonance. But this is only a coping mechanism to avoid the long-term pitfalls of dissonance. You have to make a focused effort to stay out of this phase. It will happen all of the time. It is real; it should not be treated like a one-day cold. It can occur daily, monthly, weekly, or for years. I want you to recognize when it is hitting you in the face.

Once you realize it, you need to be committed to making a real effort to correct it. I will show you ways to get out of it later in the book, but for now, recognize it and commit to change.

Reflection Questions: Take a look at your work schedule. Answer these questions for yourself:

- **How many hours a day do you spend at work?**
- **How many hours a week do you spend at work?**
- **How many hours a month do you spend at work?**
- **How many hours a day do you spend on yourself?**
- **How many hours a week do you spend on yourself?**
- **How many hours a month do you spend on yourself?**
- **How many hours a day do you spend with your family?**
- **How many hours a week do you spend with your family?**
- **How many hours a month do you spend with your family?**

Take your responses and write them down. When you get to the chapter on the 24-Hour Formula, you will need them.

#worklife #familylife #personaltime #michaelalaidler

NOTES

_____

_____

_____

_____

_____

_____

_____

_____

_____

_____

_____

_____

_____

_____

_____

_____

_____

_____

_____

_____

_____

_____

Next Life Cycle

"Every next level of your life will demand a different you."

—*Leonardo eDiCaprio*

Truly living your purpose means constantly evolving into the next level of your life. Your purpose is not a destination; it is not a one-and-done thing you can check off a list. As you continually grow, your purpose grows with it.

In 2017, I was sitting at my desk in my home office when I realized my life was continuously changing. Something in me said, "Change is for the best."

As I was thinking about this, I was scrolling through Facebook when I saw a post from a friend and former coworker. He had posted a quote that said, "Success is the maximum utilization of the ability you have." This quote intrigued me. Another post showed him standing on a stage wearing a gray suit and holding a microphone. Another showed him standing in front of a sign that said the John Maxwell Team. This interested me to the point

where I had to give him a call to understand what he was doing in his life.

When we got on the phone, I had to say, "Man, you're looking really sharp. What are you doing in life nowadays?" And he said with his normal friendly voice, "I joined the John Maxwell Team."

He explained he had got certified as a coach, trainer, and speaker. He said he enjoyed the program so much he was going to use it to jump-start his own speaking business. He provided me with the website and told me to go check it out.

Since I already knew that I wanted to learn more about leadership and it felt like it was time for me to start preparing for my next life cycle, I checked out the website.

I reached out to them and a strategy call was set up. The next thing I knew, I was signed up for the John Maxwell Team (for a fee, of course).

I wasn't sure what I was getting into, but I knew I would learn about leadership. It helped start me moving in the right direction in a lot of areas in my life.

In August 2017, I went to the John Maxwell Team certification, which was held in Florida, and I discovered what I needed to do to maximize my purpose: I had to focus on myself first, then I could focus on everyone else. That was one of the reasons I opened my speaking business. I interacted with so many people who wanted to improve themselves. I had never experienced this type of energy before. I learned from all of them how much time I quickly needed to invest in my own personal growth as well as the

leadership development of others. Two months after I went through the certification program, I formed Michael Laidler, LLC. Now it is called Michael Laidler Unlimited.

After creating my own speaking business, I realized that I was not prepared to take on this big task. It was not because I could not do the work, but being a part of someone else's business and running your own business are completely two different things.

I had to go back to the drawing board and consider the actions I needed to take in order to make it a profitable business. I felt like no matter how many books I read, I just could not get the answer I was looking for.

I needed help. To get to the next level in my life, I needed to be willing to ask for help. Don't be afraid to reach out to mentors to help you along the way.

One of the many advantages of the John Maxwell Team was that it showed me how to not only become a mentor to others but also how to use them to increase my skill set.

I had to learn that mentors are important to anyone's life, no matter what phase you're in, but especially as you enter a new life cycle. Mentors are important because they are leaders who have already done what you're trying to do. It is always best to find a mentor who is one or two levels above where you are currently at; if you're entry-level, you don't want the CEO as your mentor, as they may have a harder time relating to where you are right now.

The tricky part about getting a mentor is understanding how to be a mentee. In John Maxwell's life, he explained

how when he was coming up as a leader, he did something that really helped springboard the people who met with him. He said that he took a hundred leaders to lunch. And this was no simple lunch. It was a lunch where he had prepared questions to ask them. He took them to lunch to pick their brains.

John Maxwell offered something of value—lunch— before asking for something of value—their knowledge. You have to do something that allows you to show you respect their knowledge and their time.

Think about your time. Think about how valuable you consider the information you have gathered over the last one, five, or twenty-five years of your life.

How would you feel if someone just came up to you and asked you if you could be their mentor, especially a person you have little to no prior knowledge of? You have to invest in yourself to show others you're worth being invested in. You may not use the same approach as John Maxwell. You need to consider your next life cycle in the same way John Maxwell did early on in his leadership career.

It may take you enrolling in their learning program as a coach, trainer, or speaker. It may take you volunteering for their organization. It may even take you following them on social media and sharing their content. Whatever it is, you must be willing to do the work to show that you are serious about wanting them as a mentor.

Let's imagine you get a mentor.

Now what?

For starters, schedule a date and time to meet. You can meet using a variety of media forms or in person; don't restrict yourself to any specific form of media because everyone has busy schedules. You have to be flexible.

In person is always the best form of communication. It allows you to read the non-verbal and verbal cues of the person. Thus, you will experience the emotions from the person's words much more when you meet in person. I would aim for this method over anything else. It is hands down the best way to connect with people. The main drawback is it is the most time-consuming type of communication. You have to add additional factors like the time it takes to travel between destinations as well as any travel delays. When every minute counts, you have to look at all external factors.

Virtual is similar to in-person communication. It offers you the opportunity to have a mentor anywhere on this planet where there is an internet connection. The biggest drawback is a person can get easily distracted when they are virtual. I know when I do virtual presentations, I have a higher chance of becoming distracted. If the doorbell rings or my cell phone goes off, it's a lot easier to look at it when someone's not sitting directly in front of me.

The phone is probably the quickest form of communication. People always have their phone on them. It also offers a verbal and text option. I am not sold on using text as a form of growth, but I understand its use because it can get to a person quicker than any other form

of communication. However, the phone has a similar drawback as virtual communication because it allows distractions to easily overtake whoever is on the other line.

Finally, email is the last form of communication I would use to connect with my mentor. But if your mentor and your desired career are heavy on email communication, this might be perfect for the two of you. Some careers require a lot of email time, and if your mentor's career falls into this category, then those exchanges can be quicker for them to see. It also offers a tracking system for your communication. You can recall the written conversation much better than trying to guess or remember what was said during your verbal meeting. However, words can easily be taken out of context or misinterpreted because of your writing style.

Once you have a set time and date, work on your questions for your mentor. Your time is important to you, and their time should also be important to you. Engage them early and throughout your time together. Remember, it is about you learning from them because they have already done it. Well-thought-out questions will allow you to steer the conversation in the direction you want, and it shows them you have prepared for the meeting. I learned from John Maxwell to always bring these questions to the initial conversation:

- What is the greatest lesson you have learned?
- What life experience stood out to you the most?
- Which interaction led you to who you are?

You can seek a potential mentor's wisdom. You may be impressed with how many of their life experiences will relate to you. From personal to work experiences, a mentor can provide you with insight in multiple areas of your life.

Some things I like to ask my mentors[2]:

How has failure shaped your life? All successful people have had failures in life. Failure affects everyone. You want to learn how they overcame their failure and made it to where they are and how their attitude shapes their responses to bad times.

What are you learning? This gives you something to research and learn.

Who can you introduce me to? Referrals are beneficial in any organization and any environment.

What have you read that I should read? A reading list is always helpful in developing your growth. The more you read, the more you know.

What have you done that I should do? You will be able to look for more experiences from this question. We all need a nudge in the right direction. This may be as simple as attending a conference you have never heard of.

How can I add value to you? This is your chance to reciprocate what your mentor has offered you. You will be surprised how many people only take and never give back. You will set yourself apart with this question.

---

2. Adapted from: John C. Maxwell, Good Leaders Ask Great Questions: Your Foundation for Successful Leadership (New York: Center Street, 2014).

Then create different questions for future meetings. You always want to do a little research before getting to the meeting with your mentor. If there is any follow-up information from your prior meeting, circle back on it.

DO's and DON'Ts for Maximizing Time with Your Mentor

DO's	DON'Ts
Focus on what your mentor receives from the relationship	Focus only on yourself when building the relationship
Be clear on your purpose	Hide your reason for being with them
Appreciate the path your mentor had to arrive at his or her destination	Criticize how your mentor arrived at his or her destination

Here are a couple more suggestions for your time with your mentor:

It's not all about you. Yes, you are obtaining a mentor to help with your next life cycle, which will help you continually develop yourself and live out your purpose; however, you are using their time to do it. People are turned off when they believe any relationship is one-sided. If you meet with them and never show any interest in their goals or life issues, it will be tougher for them to focus on your growth. So ask them questions about themselves. Be interested in their life even when it doesn't always apply to you. You have to make it consistently clear how much you appreciate their sacrifice to be with you.

Focus on clarity. From day one of your partnership with a mentor, be clear on your purpose. You have to tell your mentor your purpose for being with them. For example, I could say to a prospective mentor, "I would like you to be my mentor because I am building a speaking business and respect how you have built your company." There is no need to sugarcoat your purpose for approaching them. When you establish a reason on day one, it allows both of you to move in the same direction immediately. It also fosters respect because we respect people more when they are up front with their intentions.

Keep your opinions to yourself about how they got to their destination. Whether or not you agree with their choices, it is not a time to be judgmental. You are there to listen and ask questions to see what strategies you can use to become better. Some strategies will work for you, while others do not apply to your goals. That is fine. You do not have to tell them what doesn't apply to you. Just listen.

The next phase of mentorship is understanding the frequency and the number of times you meet. When I am a mentee, I like to set monthly meetings for twelve months. This allows me to digest our last meeting and prepare for the next one. It gives me time to grow from the lessons my mentor has provided to me.

I like to have these meetings from thirty minutes to one hour. Anything less than thirty minutes would not allow me to go deep into my questions. Anything more than an hour would stretch my mentor's time.

Your journey into living out your purpose is a never-ending process. When you get a mentor, get another one in a separate area of your life. I have had leadership mentors, marketing mentors, religious mentors, family mentors, you name it. I have discovered I can always learn from someone's experiences. I have always been a fan of learning from others in order for me to mimic the good or stay away from the bad. It's no benefit to you to learn the rough way. Mentors help you as you prepare for your next life cycle.

Reflection Question: When will you get a mentor? If you have had one before, what did you learn from them?

#mentor #mentorship #michaelalaidler

Key Points for Self-Awareness

★ To live out your purpose, you need to know why you are developing yourself.

★ You have to stay consistent and committed to building people's awareness of you.

★ It is important to understand dissonance can happen at any time. Be prepared for it.

★ Seek out ways to show your skill set.

★ Find a mentor.

NOTES

Key 3: The Path to Greatness

"It isn't what we say or think that defines us, but what we do."

—Jane Austen

I am a big basketball fan. I have enjoyed basketball since the Jordan era in the '90s. I particularly enjoyed the time when Kobe Bryant was in the league. From day one, I was impressed by his work ethic. From an early age, he explained, he was not the fastest, strongest, or most talented kid on his team. One year in summer league when he was a teenager, he did not score any points during the entire summer. To him, that was a failure. He could not believe he did not score one point. He took that failure as a driving force to practice his jump shots, dribbling, and defense daily. He continued the same process throughout his entire career because it was his way to grow and be the

best version of himself, and he had realized he was going to have to work harder than everybody else in order to achieve his goals.

I watched him play at a professional level for twenty years for the Los Angeles Lakers. That is a lot of years to be successful in a physically demanding sport. Yet, he did not allow the skills he had created early on to minimize the challenges he would face later in life when it came to basketball. He kept pushing himself and finding ways to grow. It was his desire to grow that set him on the path to greatness.

From my observations, there are a lot of Kobe Bryants in the world. They have high expectations. They have strong work ethics. But unlike Kobe, they are missing the strategies to get there and maintain their own level of self-awareness. Over the next few chapters, we will explore a few strategies you can use to increase your self-awareness and get on the path to greatness.

Reflection Question: What strategies are you using to maximize your journey and be the best version of yourself?

What to Expect in this Key

The Path to Greatness

Teams

New Strategies

Renewal

The 24-Hour Formula

Teams

"A player who makes a team great is more valuable than a great player. Losing yourself in the group, for the good of the group—that's teamwork. The star of the team is the team."

—*John Wooden*

Being in law enforcement for seventeen years, I have been on a lot of teams. In some teams, I was the leader; in others, I was a member. When you have only been a member of a team, you never really understand the role of leadership and don't always look at how what you do impacts the leader. A good leader knows they are surrounded by different types of players who can determine their success or failure as a leader.

For me to succeed as a leader and thrive on my path to greatness, I had to pay attention to what made me a good team member and analyze what a good team member looked like. The main attribute that I found to be consistent in all of my teams was communication. Without

communication, I could not understand the mission of the team. This meant I had to listen to the leader. I had to be open to new ideas from the person I was following. If I could not listen to my leader, then my team would not have the same drive to listen to me when I was in the leadership role.

One of the first times that I can remember being an official leader, where the results rested solely on my shoulders, was when I became president of the local Toastmasters Club in Pineville, Louisiana. I did not realize how much my decision-making, or lack thereof, would influence the direction of the club.

For those who have never participated in Toastmasters, it is an educational organization designed to increase your leadership and public speaking abilities. The members— including the officers, like the president, vice president, treasurer, and secretary—are all volunteers.

In John Maxwell's book *The 21 Irrefutable Laws of Leadership*, he says the hardest people to lead are your peers and volunteers. I completely agree. When I was asked to be the president of that particular Toastmasters Club, I had no experience running a Toastmasters Club. I had joined Toastmasters only a few months before.

After a few months, I realized my success was being dictated by the members of the club because as the president, I had to increase membership and achieve goals outlined in the Distinguished Club Program.

I was fortunate enough to have two senior members in the club with me, Jerry "Jay" McKinney and Kimberly

Boyd. They were both a wealth of knowledge and supported the goals of the program. Without them, it did not matter how good my leadership skills were, I would not have been able to have a successful year with the club. As I compared Dr. Maxwell's book and my experience leading volunteers, I recognized the importance of understanding who I was as a leader. I understood how being aware of my delegation skills and my trusting abilities would give Jay and Kim the opportunity to help build me up as the president of that club.

I understood that as the president I could have easily made every decision on my own. I could have told them what to do and how to do it. But that would not have been a smart choice.

I thrived because I followed a few tips I learned about self-awareness and having a team around me:

- Assume my teammates are providing me with feedback for my gain
- Talk to my teammates, not about them
- Care about their success as much as I care about my own
- Push them to do their best

Let's look at the first tip. You have to assume your teammates are providing you with feedback for your gain. No one likes assumptions, but continually questioning your teammates' intent creates distrust. Trust starts with the leader. If you believe your team is out to get you, you will never be able to establish trust. You will always be

looking over your shoulders or trying to find an ulterior motive as to why your team is saying what they are, and your team will sense your distrust toward them.

Believe in your team unless they give you a reason not to. With most teams I have worked with, I believed they were providing me with feedback that was in my best interest. If I found myself looking for the negatives in what they were saying to me, I would always see the negative. If I approached their feedback in a positive manner, I was more receptive to applying it. And it was through the application of the feedback that I was able to discover more about myself as an individual and a leader. When we have this open line of feedback, it increases trust.

In the book *The 10 Laws of Trust*, Joel Peterson explains how a leader must communicate with his team. Communication is a two-way street. You must provide them with feedback and be willing to accept feedback from them as well.

Whenever Jay or Kim provided me feedback on how I was performing as president, I accepted they were doing it with my best interest in mind. Kim was especially good at giving feedback in a positive manner; she had nearly twenty years in Toastmasters. I may not always have wanted to hear it, but it was right for my own growth as an individual and leader. I grew because I kept my ears open to their advice.

Tips I follow

With My Team:

- Assume my teammates are providing me with feedback for my gain.
- Talk to my teammates, not about them.
- Care about their success as much as I care about my own.
- Push them to do their best.

The second tip is to talk to teammates, not about them. Gossip is a killer in all environments. If you create an environment which promotes gossip, the team around you will lose trust in you. More importantly, they will lose the ability to trust you enough to tell you about yourself. As an individual, if you have any negative remarks to say about someone, keep them to yourself or tell the person directly about it. I know it is not easy to do, but your team will have more respect for you when you talk directly to them rather than about them. Remember that negative news travels quicker than positive news. If it's negative, keep it to yourself. If it is positive, let everyone know about it.

The third tip is to care about your team's success as much as you care about your own. The old saying goes, "People do not care about you until they know how much you care about them." This is very accurate when it comes to human relationships. The more you show your care in

helping them succeed, the more they will want to help you succeed.

I recognized this tip when I began my speaking business. At first, I found myself always asking people for help. I would ask things like, "Can you share this on social media for me?" or "Do you have any referrals?" and "What do you think about my photo?" I was asking for their time and attention. I assumed they would help because they were a family member, a friend, or a close acquaintance. I did not know how important it was to help them first.

When my speaking business grew at a snail's pace, I wondered what was going on. I had to reflect on what I was doing. I learned I was not caring about others' success as much as I cared about my own. After I learned my weakness in this area, I would go out of my way to help others accomplish their dreams and goals. By doing this, I saw it come back to me at two and three times the speed. People saw I cared for them and they reciprocated by caring more for me.

Just like with a bank account, you need to make deposits in order to make withdrawals. In this case, your time and attention are the money. The more you deposit, the more you will have in the bank. When you truly need something from others, you can make a withdrawal. Your ability to show care first starts with you. And then, it can be completed by others.

I always told Jay how much I wanted him to succeed in Toastmasters. There was never any doubt about what I was trying to accomplish for him. I recognized his success was my success. If he did well, I did well.

The fourth tip is to push them to do their best. This is why I like working out with other people. Whenever I work out with another person, I find myself going a little harder and completing one extra rep on the bench press when I am already exhausted. I find them pushing me because I pushed them to come to the gym with me.

In Toastmasters, I constantly pushed Jay to complete more speaking assignments. It led to him earning his Distinguished Toastmasters Award at a faster pace. He showed his appreciation for me by pushing me to complete my Distinguished Toastmaster Award, which I finished in 2020. Pushing someone else to be better resulted in me becoming better. Since he pushed me, it helped me grow my leadership and speaking abilities more quickly than if I had done it on my own. Undoubtedly, it made me more efficient in my speaking business.

When I continued to use these tips throughout my tenure as a member and president of Toastmasters that year, I created a group of people I knew had each other's back. As a group, we all trusted, supported, and challenged each other to do our best. Based on these factors, I was honored when we earned the President's Distinguished Club award, which is the highest award a club can get. Since we were all on the same page, it allowed me to increase my self-awareness because I saw the strategy of believing in others worked.

Reflection Question: What strategies are you using to build trust in your team?

#teamwork #trust #michaelalaidler

NOTES

_____

_____

_____

_____

_____

_____

_____

_____

_____

_____

_____

_____

_____

_____

_____

_____

_____

_____

_____

_____

_____

_____

_____

_____

New Strategies

"It's to constantly try to be the best version of yourself.
It's a constant quest to try to be better today
than you were yesterday."

—*Kobe Bryant*

They say, "You cannot teach an old dog a new trick." I am not sure if that is true or not. I know people can improve when they want to understand their life and the ongoing changes around them. In 2017 when I separated from my wife, I realized I needed a new strategy. I didn't want to learn and use new strategies, but it was clear that what I was doing wasn't working. When life gives you lemons, make lemonade. I quickly learned I had to incorporate a couple of the following strategies in order to understand what was going on with my life.

If you want to reach greatness, you too will need to use these strategies.

First strategy: listen and communicate. It sounds very easy to do, but we rarely really do it. We usually

listen and communicate to be understood and rarely do we listen and communicate to understand. We also tend to hear what we want to hear instead of what is really being said. When it came to listening and communicating, I had to learn to never assume I understood what people were thinking or saying to me. This was not easy. Due to my heavy background in law enforcement, I still assume a lot about situations. I work on myself in this area all of the time. Nowadays, I always think of clarifying questions to understand who, what, where, when, why, and how something is happening rather than assume something based on my perspective. I do not have to agree with people's viewpoints; however, I do need to sincerely listen and understand them the best I can.

When I am trying to clarify something said to me, I will ask:

What is the purpose behind this? First, I ask myself this question. I put myself in the person's situation to determine if I understand their viewpoint based on my own life experiences. Second, I will ask the person this question to understand how important the topic is to him or her. This minimizes guessing if the topic is important to the person. The more I know about its importance, the more I can understand their passion behind it.

What else am I missing? After the person explains the purpose of the statement, I look for more facts. I want to have as much information as possible. In the past, I have learned when I ask this question, it makes the person think more about details they want me to know.

I experienced this question the first time I had a personal coach. During one of my coaching sessions, my coach asked, "What else am I missing?" I responded, "Yes, I forgot to tell you . . ." This made me think more deeply about what I was trying to convey to my coach.

Remember, everyone has life experiences that are different from ours. They may forget to add the additional information because they believe they answered your question thoroughly during the initial question about purpose. But they don't always, and it helps to ask follow-up questions, so they can fill in the blanks for you. Especially when the question is about them.

Is this what you said to me? It is tough to go wrong when you paraphrase what someone said to you. It helps you confirm what the person said, and it lets them know you are listening to them.

Listen and Communicate

Ask Yourself These Questions

What is the purpose behind this?	What else am I missing?	Is this what you said to me?

As you improve these listening skills, it will improve

your ability to communicate. In Stephen Covey's book *The 7 Habits of Highly Effective People*, he talks about empathetic listening. In empathic listening, you are listening with your entire self. You are going past the words you hear. You are watching their eyes to see their body language and behavior. Your heart senses the meaning and feelings behind their words.

For example, when a person looks directly in my eyes while talking about a topic they are passionate about, it creates a verbal and visual connection with me. I can feel the person's passion through their body language. I am not implying that if the person does not look me directly in the eyes they are not passionate about the topic, but it is one way to convey this.

Second strategy: reflection. I learned how to reflect on my past experiences and how to use them to my benefit. I am not saying I wanted to experience some of the things I have, but I'm fortunate to be able to have learned from them. My reflection time allowed me to look at the situations I was in and how I and others behaved. Even to this day, I still do things that make me question my actions, but because I'm using the power of reflection, I know I can improve on them.

I reflect daily. Typically, I reflect at night once my day is over. I look at all of the activities I experienced and determine how they impacted my life. I will pay attention to what I accomplished and what I did not finish. For the activities I did not finish, I review them to determine why

I did not complete them.

For example, if I did not finish my daily goal of personal development, I ask myself, "What activities kept me from completing my personal development?" Then, I review all of the other activities for the day. As I look through the other activities, I reduce or eliminate the time I spend doing them and add the additional time to my personal development for the next day. So if I spent one hour on social media that day, I will only spend thirty minutes on it the next day. The remaining thirty minutes will be spent on personal development. As you reflect daily, you will find all types of time you can maximize to focus on your own personal development.

Third strategy: think before you act. I have not always used this strategy in my life. I am sure my friends and family can attest to it. I really had to think before I acted, given my primary career involved law enforcement.

I was a hard charger who jumped straight into the fire, but on the job, I had to make sure I did not respond in a way that was too impulsive. I had to eliminate knee-jerk reactions because they could cost me my life.

I learned that not using my brain caused issues for me and those around me. As life went on and I used some of the other strategies like reflection, I benefited from knowing what triggered me and what I had to do to minimize how quickly I reacted.

These are strategies I have learned to use to help me think before I act:

1. Slow down—Certain decisions in your life do not have to be rushed. If you can wait on taking action, then wait for it. Not everything is a sprint in life.

2. Deep breath—Take a deep breath before responding to something that upsets you. This will help you stop the first reckless words that come out of your mouth. Allow air to flow before your words can flow.

3. Write it down—I learned this from Abraham Lincoln's book *Lincoln on Leadership*. When Lincoln experienced negative behaviors towards him, he did not respond immediately. He would write his response down on a piece of paper and place it in his desk drawer. He would leave it there for the night. The next day he would retrieve the paper, and if he felt the same way, he would send it to the person. Most of the time, he did not feel the same way and never sent the letter. You can do this in your cell phone's notes application. Leave it there until the next morning. If you feel the same way, text it to the person. If you do not feel the same way, delete it. I have used this response many times. Fortunately, I rarely send the response the next day. This tactic has saved many relationships because I realized two negative responses do not equal a positive response. It works, trust me.

On the other hand, if you do not think before you act and say or do something that is negative, it is not the end of

the world. Once you have responded in a negative manner and realize your actions, you can apologize for doing it. An apology will go far. It will go far for the other person and you. An apology will show you are taking ownership of your actions.

I would rather make a mistake, apologize for it, and work on fixing something I know I should not have done, versus making the mistake and trying to overlook it. You may not fully repair the relationship but it will show the person you cared enough to make the effort and put you on the right track for making things right again.

Fourth strategy: search for lessons. This is similar to reflection. But it is reflection with purpose. As you reflect on situations in your life, ask, "What can I learn from this?"

When I was a police officer, due to my high level of energy, I found myself pushing the envelope on multiple occasions. One night I was working at one of the local clubs in Tallahassee. This was a usual night of loud music and packed parking lots. It was near the closing time of the club. As this particular night progressed, I caught a purple Dodge Magnum in a traffic violation. I turned on my overhead lights and attempted to stop the vehicle. The vehicle sped away. The police department's pursuit policy was pretty strict: unless it was a violent felony, pursuits were not authorized. As the vehicle fled, I lost sight of it and did not know where it went. I continued with my evening. I looked around for the vehicle and, eventually, saw it pulling out of a bank parking lot.

Given the time and the vehicle, I knew it was the same one that had fled from me earlier. I attempted a second time to initiate a traffic stop in my patrol vehicle. Once again, the car took off. I saw the vehicle pull into a dead-end area and all the passengers bail out of the vehicle. All four passengers ran in different directions. The main person I wanted was the driver.

I stopped my vehicle, put it in park, locked the door, and began a foot chase behind the driver. The driver ran across the intersection, which was four lanes with a median in the middle. Fortunately, no vehicles were coming from either direction. He jumped a fence into a backyard, and I lost sight of him. As a young police officer, I was still pretty athletic and in shape, so I jumped into the backyard too. It was extremely dark at night and the neighborhood had very few lights. I decided to continue looking for the driver in the backyard, but I lost sight of him. I did not believe I was going to find him. After about a minute, I saw his head behind a trash can. I told him to put his hands behind his back, he complied, and I was able to place handcuffs on him. I got lucky I did not get hurt chasing after someone in the dark for a minor traffic violation.

I learned from the experience. I learned not everything is worth it. I needed to place a value on my worth. As I got deeper into my law enforcement career, one of the main lessons I learned from that experience was that although nothing bad happened, a lot of bad things could have happened. The car could have hit a pedestrian. The driver could have been hit by a car when he was running across

the street. I could have injured myself jumping over the fence. I could have been assaulted and possibly killed in someone's backyard.

There's always a lesson to be learned in everything we do. It doesn't matter if it was a good or bad experience because you are going to learn something from whatever you have done. Searching for a lesson allows you to continuously grow throughout your life and keeps you from only analyzing the bad part of what happened, as it helps to highlight the good parts as well. Remember, failure is going to happen no matter what we do. It is up to us how we respond to it.

Fifth strategy: free up time. People always tease me because of my ability to free up my time. When I say free up time, I really mean delegate. You only have twenty-four hours a day and seven days a week. Delegation can be tricky when it involves you. Typically, I find that when anything involves me directly, I need to do it. I need to be the person to have my hands directly involved in my growth.

In theory, though, it is a great idea. I talk about delegation in my presentation called Developing the Law Enforcement Officer Within You. Being able to delegate takes your growth to the next level. Many small tasks, like managing your social media or cooking a meal, can be outsourced to somebody else. When you are on an extensive personal growth journey, sometimes you have to delegate some of the basics.

The first time I had to delegate anything was when I began my business. I thought I had enough time to grow my LinkedIn, Instagram, and Facebook accounts. I thought I had enough time to make phone calls daily. I thought I could manage my books. I thought I could do it all while holding a full-time job.

But I realized these tasks were eating into my reading and reflection time. I had to change, so I reached out to The Business Club Academy, a marketing company that is operated by Adam Flores. You can find more information about them at https: //www.thebusinessclubacademy. com/.

By using them to manage my social media, I could refocus my energy on myself. I became more aware of the areas I needed to improve on. Yes, it did come at a monetary cost, but the benefits of spending my time on myself outweighed the cost.

Don't be afraid to outsource tasks. The money spent is an investment in yourself.

Sixth strategy: start small. When I started writing this book, I thought I had to write the entire manuscript in two days. I learned quickly, through the Self-Publishing School, that you have to take it one chapter at a time. And as you move forward, you gradually gain momentum. I felt my momentum skyrocket at ten thousand words. If I had not started small and instead tried to write all the chapters in one day, I would have crushed myself.

Another example of starting small would be if you are trying to run a marathon. To run that many miles in one

day, you have to spend months building your body up to be able to withstand that kind of physical stress. You have to start small to achieve the long-term effects. Self-awareness is a lifelong and continuous process, which has to be taken in small segments.

To start small, implement this process:

1. Look at one goal for increasing your self-awareness. Go back to the Goals chapter and use the SMART framework to begin the process.
2. Break down the goal into tasks.
3. List each step in the task.
4. As you complete each step, cross it off. Do not move on to the next step until the prior one has been completed.
5. After all of the steps are crossed off, go to the next task.
6. When you look at your steps and tasks and everything is crossed off, your goal will be complete.

Let's imagine your goal will be to earn a promotion in your organization. It does not happen only because you want it. You will have to complete certain tasks in order to make yourself eligible for the position. You might need to:

• Research the position description.
• Review your own resume and compare it to the position requirements.
• For experience you do not have, develop the additional experience (e.g., take a leadership

course, complete a six-month internship, pass a position-specific certification exam, etc.).
- Fill out the position application.
- Interview for the position.
- Wait for the decision.

Now, we have a few tasks that might be required for the promotion. What's next? You need to break down the first task into steps. In order to research the position description, you will need to review the following:

- Job Qualifications
- Job Responsibilities
- Job Duties

Reviewing each step will prepare you for the next one. But you cannot skip any step before going to the next one. If you do, you will find yourself going backward and wasting time. Remember, complete the step, cross it off, then move on to the next step in the task. Once all of the steps are complete, then you are ready for the next task. After all of the tasks are complete, you will have accomplished your goal.

I know this may seem a little tedious. But I always think about a quote from Theodore Roosevelt when it comes to spending a lot of time on things I feel are important to me. He said, "Nothing worth having was ever achieved without effort." If you want to accomplish life-changing goals, they will take work and effort.

Seventh strategy: rebuild your network. Jim Rohn said, "You are the average of the five people you

spend the most time with." You do not have to have a lot of people to grow yourself. Your five people will influence your growth, your income, and how you view yourself. If they are positive and want to see you grow, you will benefit. It is important to think about who in your life builds you up and who is taking away from your potential. This may sound tough, but it is your level of self-awareness that will dictate your efficiency as a person.

When I went through my divorce a few years ago, I had to understand who was in my network. I could not call on everyone and anyone. I realized certain people would provide me with the support I needed; the other people would provide me with negativity, which would slow my growth and make me go backward more than go forward. I had to consciously reach out to people I trusted who would help me build my self-awareness. When you are building or rebuilding your network, ask yourself the following questions:

- *What do they bring to my life*? It is always best to surround yourself with people who will strengthen your weakness. If they cannot add value, there is no purpose for that person to be around you.
- *What do I bring to their life*? You have to care about them, too. You cannot have a one-way street to your growth. You have to provide them with growth as well.
- *What are they willing to give*? For me, time is important. Having someone simply listen to my

issues helps me release my stress. I need a friend or two to hear me ramble about the fun and crappy parts of my day.

After you ask yourself these questions, you may find some people in your network do not meet your criteria. I recommend having a conversation with the person. A conversation about expectations will be impactful to you and the other person. Tell the person what you are aiming to achieve in your life and give them the chance to understand what success looks like to you. If this does not work or the person does not care, tell the person where they sit with you going forward. You will have to explain how much time you cannot spend with them going forward. This will never be an easy conversation. It even seems harsh. However, you have to have this conversation with the person. After all, it is what you would expect from others. You only have so much time in your life, and you need to spend it with people who have your best interest in mind.

To meet people who meet your criteria, you can start where most people spend their time: at work. The next time you are at work, look for people who are positive, driven, and want to be successful. You might even know a few people like that right now. If you do, write their names somewhere. I am going to make it even easier. Write down one person's name on the line below:

Now, go up to this person and ask the following questions:

- What are your goals?
- Where do you see yourself in six months? One year? Ten years?
- How much time do you spend growing the people around you?

These types of questions show how people think about their future. If it aligns with what you are doing, create more conversations to see if you can grow together. If it does not, it is okay. There are more people out there. You can continue to look for more people. Keep in mind, you need to make sure you have your own answers to those questions, as the person will likely want to know your answers as well.

Rebuild Your Network

Ask Yourself These Questions

What do they bring to my life?

What do I bring to their life?

What are they willing to give?

These are a lot of strategies to consider. And they are all feasible. I know if I can do them, you can as well. I have gone through my life executing them and reaping their benefits. It was not always easy, but I never told you it would be easy to be great. I learned to use each strategy as building blocks for my life. If you are already implementing these strategies, keep working on them because I know the results will come to you.

Reflection Question: Which strategy best suits you?

#strategy #michaelalaidler

NOTES

_____

_____

_____

_____

_____

_____

_____

_____

_____

_____

_____

_____

_____

_____

_____

_____

_____

_____

_____

_____

Renewal

"Rest when you are weary. Refresh and renew yourself,
your body, your mind, your spirit.
Then get back to work."

—Ralph Marston

Nathan was your prototypical worker. He worked long hours, showing up to work early and staying late. He produced results for his organization, was loyal to the company, and believed in the company's mission and vision. He was on the path to becoming his organization's next chief executive officer. At home, he had the perfect family. He loved his wife. His children performed well in school. They enjoyed family vacations often and maintained a healthy relationship with their church. On the outside, everything seemed perfect about Nathan's life.

But looks were deceiving. Nathan spent too much time at work, and the line between home and work life was

blurred. While his results were high for years, they started to decline. Nathan entered into a pattern where he could no longer realize the difference between himself and his organization.

Eventually, he tried to take even more family vacations and less work. Those were only temporary fixes because they did not provide a long-term solution for his issue. It was too late. All of the years he spent focusing hours and hours on his organization without focusing on himself and his family had finally hit a boiling point. His wife was upset, and his relationship with his children was strained. He realized he had a problem. He realized he had slipped into dissonance.

Earlier, we talked about the downfalls of dissonance. Nathan exhibited all of them. One of the pitfalls with dissonance is most people do not know they are experiencing it until they have been in it for years. They do not realize they need help. This was the exact thing that happened to Nathan. By the time he realized he was in dissonance, his wife wanted a divorce, his kids barely wanted to call him "Dad," and his work performance was sliding down. He needed something new.

This is when Nathan found the idea of renewal. For most people, renewal is a "feel-good" term—not a real thing. Although we know these techniques can help, we reject them because they are not part of the norm. In industries like law enforcement, it can make you look weak. All of the negative connotations are wrong.

Renewal is an approach that helps us slow down our thinking and gives us the chance to understand how our self-consciousness works. Three main areas are part of the renewal process: mindfulness, hope, and compassion.

Mindfulness means to be fully present in the moment. When mindfulness is high, we can improve how we think, feel, and act. We build our relationships, attitudes, and performance at work. When we are more mindful, we quickly recognize the true nature of our feelings. While this isn't always easy, the long-term effects allow you to succeed over time.

A technique I have learned to use while practicing mindfulness is the six-second method. I discovered this method after reading the article called "Just 6 seconds of mindfulness can make you more effective" by Chade-Meng Tan. Using this method is quite easy:

- Move to a quiet area
- Hold your breath for a moment
- Focus all your attention on your mind and body (close your eyes if that helps)
- Breathe in through your nose
- Internally count to six
- Release your breath

That is one round of the method. There is something magical in those six seconds that helps my mind relax and assists me in taking a step back from everything else. I repeat as needed.

Take this opportunity to try the six-second method. I recommend doing three to five rounds in the beginning to get used to it. After a few days, you can increase it to whatever you feel you need to get to your level of mindfulness.

When I am in the renewal process and the mindfulness state, I can block out all of the distractions, like a TV being on, my cell phone making noise notifications, my desire to begin another task, etc. Essentially, being in this state removes all outside distractions.

During renewal, I pinpoint areas that are positive and negative. Events that are positive, I work on increasing. If I spent time with my son, I consider how I can increase that activity. Events that are negative, I aim to keep out of my life. If I had a dispute with a coworker, I work on how I can avoid the same dispute in the future. I go back to the strategies on reflection and search for lessons, so I do not continue to have the same negative events because they increase my dissonance by creating more disharmony in my life. Positive events decrease dissonance, while negative events will increase it.

As you understand how you feel about different stimuli, you can maximize the time you spend in positive moments. We can be happier when mindfulness is addressed and emphasized.

Hope is the second area of renewal. When our mind is optimistic about the future, we have a better chance to respond in a calm manner and with poise. Hope makes it

possible for us to handle complexity, fear, frustration, and stress. Hope positively affects the mind. This is one of the important parts of having a coach or a mentor or anybody that can inspire you. The process of coaching helps bring out the positive feelings and requires us to have a vision of what is to come. As we become more hopeful, our breathing slows, our blood pressure drops, and our immune system responds more efficiently.

Another way to bring hope to your life is through vision statements. A vision statement is like a roadmap. Companies often have vision statements, and it can be a good way to check if you are really in alignment with the place you work. The downside of vision statements by our employer is that they are more about the company than about us. Whenever I look at a vision statement from a company, I determine how I can combine my own personal vision statement with the company's mission statement. If we do not believe in the same principles, we would never be able to honor what the company is attempting to do. Just like a company's vision statement, our own vision statement encourages us to design a path to success. It encourages us to have solid and measurable actions that are tied to how we want to live.

Sometimes people shy away from writing out a personal vision statement because they worry that if they do not accomplish their goals, they will be disappointed. But studies show that you are way more likely to accomplish the goals that you write down. Seeing your goals written down will help you see what you can (and will) do in the

future. It gives you a visual idea of what to look forward to. Thus hope, along with written goals, will bring positive aspirations, which ultimately reduces dissonance.

Compassion is the third area of renewal. Compassion is for yourself and others. The reality is everyone goes through multiple crises. "Everyone" includes you. We all experience some level of burnout or have a hard time with the work-life balance, so it's essential to have compassion for yourself and others.

It's time to look at what is going on around you that can affect how you feel and react. This is not the time to make excuses. I do not want you to try to downplay how something is making you feel. If you are making excuses or saying "everything's fine" when it's not, you are not being compassionate with yourself.

As you become more compassionate with yourself, you will have more patience and perseverance, you will be viewed positively by those around you, and you will form a stronger social bond and build relationships. To strengthen your compassion, do three activities.

Activity 1: Take a moment to see yourself. You could do this while practicing the six-second mindfulness method. If the six-second method is not enough, enter into meditation. If you've never done any type of meditation, go to Google or YouTube and find a self-guided version that works for you. I would start with a five-minute meditation and gradually increase as you see fit. Taking this moment for yourself allows you to get a grasp on your emotions and place yourself first.

Activity 2: Look at your life in perspective. Consider what is going on in your life. If you are dealing with difficult circumstances, then recognize those and give yourself grace. Take the time to look around you. If you can look around you, you are still alive. You woke up this morning and are currently reading this book. If you are doing this, then you have the chance to do more. There is always potential for a better day.

Activity 3: Forgive yourself. We are so tough on ourselves. We do not see failures as mistakes. You have to forgive yourself and keep on moving. You will make another mistake; don't worry about that. All you can do is live and learn from them.

Embrace the process of renewal through mindfulness, hope, and compassion. These three areas of renewal can be completed in any order; just make sure you are doing them consistently.

When you properly address these areas, you open your thinking to what drives you. These areas help stimulate the PSNS (parasympathetic nervous system), which controls our "rest and digest" response to stress, as they bring increased self-awareness and fight against the downfalls of stress. When the PSNS is operating effectively, your body can conserve energy, regulate bodily functions like digestion, and calm down and think. In law enforcement or any environment with elevated levels of stress, this system has to remain efficient for us to recover from long days of work. When we do not make a concentrated effort to keep the PSNS operating at the high level it is designed for, we can face detrimental illnesses.

I first learned about the effects of the PSNS when I investigated crimes as a police officer. I enrolled in a few classes at the Multijurisdictional Counterdrug Task Force Training Program, which focused on investigations and interviewing. One of the topics of these courses was how our body responds to stress. The course continually emphasized how the PSNS is one of the few areas we cannot control. Sometimes, the PSNS is affected by the duration of our stress levels. Other times, it is affected by the intensity of the stimuli.

The same thing happens with us when it comes to self-awareness. We cannot control our PSNS on a surface level. We have to devote time and energy to breaking the PSNS down and understanding what makes us tick. This is what the process of renewal offers. It offers us a chance

to look at each area that controls how much time we spend focusing on ourselves.

If you have not realized it yet, I want you to spend time focusing on yourself. You cannot become a great asset to anyone if you are not doing all you can to understand your own personality and your own character. The renewal process can be simple when you dedicate time to it.

While it took Nathan years to learn renewal, it was an activity he needed to complete for him to move forward with his life. Although he did not have a marriage anymore, he still had the opportunity to reconnect with his children. He learned there are more important things than work. He learned he had to focus on himself first. He allowed himself to be great again.

Reflection Questions: Do you know anyone like Nathan? Do you consider yourself a Nathan? If so, it is time for a renewal. You need to schedule a time when you are free of distractions and can focus on your true self.

Once you have made time for a reboot, you can focus on your day-to-day activities.

#renewal #michaelalaidler

NOTES

The 24-Hour Formula

"Do one thing at a time. Start the day with a list of things you have to do, and do the most important things first. Even if you don't get the list done, you've gotten the most important things done. So many people spend so much time on things that aren't important."

—Brian Tracy

At the end of 2017, I bought a book by Brian Tracy called *Time Management*. Before reading this book, I believed I knew a lot about time management. I was getting tasks completed on time. I thought I was efficient. I was wrong. I did not realize the importance of planning each day to get the most out of it. I was not planning what was important to me and how it affected my life. I was doing activities as they came about rather than planning for them in advance.

If you want to achieve greatness, you have to be intentional with your time.

Brian Tracy said you should dedicate sixty to ninety minutes of your time to any activity you do, as you can't accomplish anything worthwhile in less time. From that point forward, every activity I planned was at least sixty minutes long and did not exceed two hours. After a few months of implementing this new strategy, although I found myself becoming more productive, I still felt I was missing something.

Then I discovered it had to do with timing. I learned from Daniel Pink how we can maximize our creative patterns. He talked about the science behind the timing of when we should focus on different activities throughout the day. As I listened more to his presentation, he explained how there are different types of chronotypes of people. In his book *When*, he identified three types of chronotypes: larks, third birds, and owls. In short, he described larks as being most productive in the morning. The third birds are most productive in the middle of the day. The owls are most productive at the end of the day.

Statistically, people are:

Larks: 14 percent

Third Birds: 65 percent

Owls: 21 percent

This information helped me understand the importance of timing. So I unified both Brian Tracy's and Daniel Pink's ideas and discovered what I had to do next.

I came up with the 24-Hour formula. This is an easy-to-implement way to plan your time. It is designed to take into account your entire day: how much time you sleep, when

you eat, when you travel, when you are at work, when you play, and whatever else you want to do throughout the day.

Since each day we have to focus on activities to improve our self-awareness, I wanted to ensure that I could spend a certain amount of time each day working on growing myself, and given that I am most productive in the morning, I put a lot of my self-awareness time then. While this may seem weird or hard to do, I recommend spending at least 10 percent of your time on personal growth every day.

How does this break down?

Each day, spend at least 2.4 hours and up to 3 hours a day on ourselves.

Each week, spend at least 16.8 hours and up to 17 hours on ourselves.

For the month, that means spending 67.2 and up to 68 hours on ourselves.

Personal Growth Breakdown

● Day - 2.4 hours, up to 3 hours (out of 24 hours)

● Week - 16.8 hours, up to 17 hours (out of 168 hours)

● Month - 67.2 hours, up to 68 hours (out of 672 hours)

For each day, three hours may seem a lot. But you do not have to do this all at once. You should have it in sixty-

minute increments unless you can do all three hours at once.

The whole point is to dedicate time to ensuring you are building yourself. If you are not building yourself, you will not have time to build others. Some of the different activities I have found that I include in these time frames to achieve my three hours of personal growth are reading books, reading articles, listening to audiobooks, and writing. These activities activate the creative fluids in my mind.

Determine whether you are a lark, a third bird, or an owl. Then make sure to allocate most of the 10 percent that should be spent on increasing your self-awareness during your most productive time of day.

Remember, you need a minimum of two hours spent on personal growth, and according to the Center for Disease Control and Prevention, at least seven hours of sleep every night.

So with all that information in mind, create your 24-Hour formula. Essentially, plan out what a typical 24-hour day looks like for you.

To keep it simple, I will start the formula with the time I go to bed each night, which is 9:30 p.m.

I have a setting on my phone which notifies me at 9:15 p.m. that I have to start relaxing because as soon as 9:30 comes around, my eyes are closed. All of the lights and electronics are turned off. My phone blocks off all notifications except ones from my family.

At 4:30 a.m., my alarm goes off. Although I want to hit the snooze button five times, I choose not to. I brush my teeth, drink some water, and stretch for fifteen to twenty minutes.

At 5:00 a.m., I begin working on professional development. Since I am a lark, I put my first professional development time in the morning, my most productive time of day. During this time, I work on new content or read. The new content is based on my goals. For example, when I was writing this book, I spent this time conducting research on the topics I was writing about as well as writing the book. If I was preparing for a presentation, I would spend this time working on its lesson plan and training aids (like the PowerPoint).

At 6:30 a.m., I get dressed and leave my house for work. I arrive at work anywhere from 6:50 a.m. to 7:30 a.m. I factor in being there anywhere from eight to ten hours. This gives me wiggle room for any unexpected activities that may come up.

Anywhere from 4:00 p.m. to 6:00 p.m., I go to the gym and work out. From 6:00 p.m. to 8:00 p.m., I take time to eat, relax my brain, and talk to my son. From 8:00 p.m. to 9:15 p.m. I utilize this time to spend with friends and family, prepare for the next day, clean up the house, and do some light reading.

This is my typical schedule Monday through Friday.

Before we move on, I hope you noticed I did not have a full 10 percent blocked off for personal development. I only had 1.5 hours.

But I actually do spend the full 10 percent and typically more. I am cognizant that any part of my day can be converted to personal development. For example, on my way to work or the gym, I can listen to audiobooks. Then at work or the gym, I make sure to have conversations with people who help me grow. Because I know the importance of this, I make sure it happens. However, in the beginning phases of your 24-Hour formula, I recommend you are intentional about dedicating time directly to your personal development.

On the weekends, my schedule changes. I sleep later and make time for church, family, and friends. Since I am not traveling to work or the gym that day, I have an additional two blocks of time reserved for personal development besides just that hour and a half during my productive time of the day.

Regardless of how your 24-Hour formula is constructed, you must make sure you plan for personal development. You have to block it out and designate the time.

In addition, make sure to allow room for distractions because they cannot be completely avoided. I add time to the above activities in my schedule to create space when needed. Although I do not believe it will always take me two hours to get off of work, go to the gym, and go back home, I have learned it is better to have extra time for myself than no time at all. In any activity I do, I prefer to be fifteen minutes early to it than one minute late. I do my best to keep distractions away, but I know I cannot dodge

them. I can prepare for them, however, and I do this with the extra time.

After you have been doing this for a while, you may find that you don't need to schedule specific one- to two-hour blocks for personal development. But even when it is not scheduled, it needs to happen with intentionality. You can find ways to incorporate personal development into the different activities you participate in. For example, when I watch TV, I try to figure out how the characters' actions contribute to different areas like leadership, decision-making, or teamwork.

The more you grow, the more you will find activities or people who will pull you away from being the best version of yourself. Do not let that happen. Instead, take control with this formula. Each time you find that you are losing your purpose and you aren't on the path to greatness, go back to the drawing board and structure a new 24-Hour formula with intention. As you plan out your schedule, remember:

- The way you manage your time will affect your rate of growth. If you take no time for yourself, then you will never see growth.
- There is no time like the present. Do not wait until tomorrow or next week. You will need to start this formula today.
- You have to control your time. If you do not plan it, someone or something else will.

Reflection Question: How will you construct your 24-Hour formula to focus on your personal development?

#24hourformula #michaelalaidler

Key Points for Self-Awareness

★ The people around you will determine your success or failure.

★ Utilize different strategies to achieve your expectations.

★ Your growth will not be easy but it will be worth it.

★ Take the time to focus on the components of renewal, which are mindfulness, hope and compassion.

★ The six-second method will help you attain mindfulness.

★ You will take control of your life by planning and implementing the 24-Hour formula.

NOTES

Conclusion

I had the *aha* moment when I realized the importance of self-awareness. I was no longer worried about my future because I started to know who I was. I utilized all of the strategies outlined in this book to build an image of myself beyond my badge. I had to take a step past my agency's title.

And when I did, I was not afraid to grow myself anymore.

As a leader, I always work hard to build up other people. I always committed to making the people around me better. Now, I have a plan that makes me better than I ever was in the past.

I hope these strategies are as impactful in your life as they are in mine.

You have to make a decision. You can choose to not follow any of these strategies and leave your self-awareness in the air. But you will become tired and upset because you remain unfocused and unable to achieve your own goals.

Or you can go after you. Yes, go after you. You can be the lion who is chasing the lion.

When you implement the steps I have outlined in this book, you will feel the effects of discovering yourself, understanding your purpose, and walking down the path to greatness.

I am excited you have taken the time to read this book. I am excited to walk along with you on your journey to self-awareness.

Let's get it!

ABOUT THE AUTHOR

Michael Laidler has worked in law enforcement for nearly two decades. He has served with distinction in numerous positions and leadership roles, from police officer, border patrol agent to federal corrections. Michael's dedication to service shines in all he does. He holds an MBA from Morehead State University, a BA from Florida State University and is a Distinguished Toastmaster. Michael has transitioned his career into training and educating law enforcement officers nationwide. A highly sought-after keynote speaker and facilitator, Michael's methods continue inspiring and developing officers to become better in every regard, especially personally. It is his goal to impart the necessary personal development skills for officers to operate at full capacity in every situation.

You can learn more at: michaelalaidler.com

Can You Help?

Thank You For Reading My Book!

I really appreciate all of your feedback, and I love hearing what you have to say.

I need your input to make the next version of this book and my future books better.

Please leave me an honest review on Amazon letting me know what you thought of the book.

Thanks so much!

Michael Laidler

447446244R00080

Made in the USA
Columbia, SC
20 October 2024

Made in the USA
Columbia, SC
09 February 2025

53192084R00052